How to Write Poetry

Mary Bishop

To Sergio

"Beauty is truth, truth beauty,—that is all
Ye know on earth, and all ye need to know."

— Ode to a Grecian Urn, John Keats

Contents

INTRODUCTION

Poetry is the way we give name to the nameless so it can be thought.

Audre Lorde, Poetry is not a Luxury

POETRY is a way of sharing dreams, desires, and fears, carving your ideas into a language. A powerful tool to construct subjectivities, poetry is not frightening or incomprehensible but it is a path to recreate ourselves.

Anybody can write poetry. It has nothing to do with where you come from, what you do, or who you are. It does not depend on your age, gender or education. As Audre Lorde points out,

> "... poetry is not a luxury. It is a vital necessity of our existence. It forms the quality of light within which we predicate our hopes and dreams toward survival and change, first made into language, then into idea, then into more tangible action." (15)

Great poems take our breath away, shake our lives, and make us feel the way we never felt before. As I recall how poetry changes our perspective about life and makes us reflect on philosophical questions, an interesting episode comes to my mind. A few years ago, during one of my poetry workshops for children, I was asking students how they felt by reading a beautiful poem. Children brought up all sorts of answers when one of them told me that he could identify a work of art when the work remained inside him forever. For this young poet, poetry provided him with a long-lasting experience, changing his form of perceiving the world.

Poetry is a way of telling stories, creating new realities through imagination and revelation. Life cannot divorce from writing and reading stories. They are part of our lives, and, most of the time, through narratives, we internalize irrelevant or degrading concepts disseminated as entertainment by media and pop culture, or in the form of knowledge, by historical narratives.

As misconceptions usually construe an angle of vision, what is told about us ends up building who we are and how we see the world, as Lugones and Spelman remark

> ... having the opportunity to talk about one's life, to give an account of it, to interpret, is integral to leading that life rather than being led through it. (17-18)

Living also means reflecting on life and poetry gives us tools to analyze our lives. Poetry is a creative form to debunk degrading ideas, bringing to light our stories and the way we see reality. *How to Write Poetry* will help you find your poetic voice, giving names to those 'ideas which are – until the poem –formless, about to be birthed, but already felt.' (Lorde,15)

This book is not a manual on how to analyze poetry, paraphrase poems or scan the accentual-syllabic verse. It will provide you with tools to understand poetry and use language to explore what seems intangible and voiceless.

The first three chapters present three sources of inspiration: memories, quotidian, ekphrasis. The first chapter focuses on remembering, a process of folding and unfolding that gives poets possibilities to use art to illuminate the past. The second explores ekphrasis, a written representation of a painting, a sculpture, or any other visual work of art. The third emphasizes how poets throw light on things, places, and situations of everyday life.

In the following chapters, I will focus on poetic language and form, such as sound, rhythm, verse, stanza, rhyme, and image.

My goal is to make you understand that poetry writing is a feasible conscious process that requires hard work and getting passionate about the creative process. Poets should be aware of the techniques and mechanisms of the craft as they sculpt their ideas and thoughts. They should know exactly what they are writing, why they are writing, and mainly, how they are writing.

BASIC STEPS

Write every day. Your first draft should be on anything that comes from your heart.

Use the stream of consciousness method, putting on paper every thought or feeling that passes through your mind. Do not ask if the first draft makes any sense, just keep going. At this point, don't interrupt any thoughts to revise your text, don't do any editing but keep writing.

Do not hide feelings. Be honest! If you are happy, celebrate it with your words. If you are anxious, stressed, or heartbroken, find a means of translating your feelings into words, sounds, colors, images, tastes.

Always have in mind that writing produces self-knowledge and you are writing for yourself. It is going to be easier to express your feelings once you learn how ambivalence, metaphors, and synesthesia can help a poet play with words to unfold experiences.

Read. You will need to find time to read a good book.

A writer has to read. A poet has to read, and if you want to be a poet, I think reading poetry is the first lesson. Start a reading diet with at least one poem a day.

Edit your work. Everything begins with the first sentences you write, then, design and edit your work carefully.

Never forget that poetry is a way of telling a story. The poetic form of saying something has to do with symbols, allegories, metaphors, and figurative language. The poet utilizes language to play a serious children's game like hide-and-seek, revealing a part of the self while hiding the other.

References

Lorde, Audre. 'Poetry is not a Luxury' in Feminist Theory edited by Wendy Kolmar and Frances Bartkowski. McGraw Hill: New York, 2005.

Lugones, Maria and Elizabeth Spelman. 'Have We Got a Theory for You' in Feminist Theory edited by Wendy Kolmar and Frances Bartkowski. McGraw Hill: New York, 2005.

Chapter 1

MEMORY AND POETRY

> I found a sanctuary... a place where I could work at explaining the hurt and making it go away.

> bell hooks, "Theory as Liberatory Practice"

WRITING is a safe house where we can reflect on life, imagine, and recreate reality. However, writing about the past is not always comfortable because it involves dealing with memories we might struggle to get rid of. Some memories resist coming out. They remain in the abyss of the mind, producing amnesia. How to express feelings and experiences we cannot remember? How to write about painful events? How to deal with suffering?

In poetry writing, when amnesia thwarts remembering, imagination comes into action, filling the gaps. By intertwining memories and imagination, poetry unveils themes that cause pain, as personal or collective experiences, and writing becomes a sanctuary. This chapter focuses on how to start writing by using your past as a source of inspiration. It concentrates on memory, and how you can access your past to write creatively. You can write about your happy moments and family celebrations, but it is also possible to turn sad moments into poetry. This exercise can help one reconcile with something unsolved. Writing can be a therapeutic exercise to heal your mind.

1.1   What is memory?

Autobiographical memories refer to our experiences and how we connect with people around us. Accessing our memories to remember what matters to us, such as the first teacher, best friends in primary school, Christmas celebrations, and so forth, can be a way of constructing subjectivity. As poems unveil what matters to us, they lead us through a road of self-discovery, a pathway to self-representation. In the end, you should write for yourself. You are your first audience.

Poets cannot write if they do not know how to represent themselves, nevertheless, learning who we are and how we deal with life and those around us become the first step to writing. Take a moment and ask yourself these questions: Who am I? What does this place mean to me? Why is this person important in my life? Am I happy with this or that? How could I change this situation? Do I make people around me happy? What hurts me? Do I hurt people unintentionally? What do I struggle to forget? Why do I enjoy remembering this?

Poets write to themselves and deal with introspection and healing before writing to an audience. In this sense, writing is like going on a journey inside us, taking a looking glass, scrutinizing every millimeter of our life without fear to reveal intimacy.

we should 'learn to bear the intimacy of scrutiny and flourish within it; as we learn to use the products of that scrutiny for power within our living, those fears which rule over us and form our silences begin to lose control over us.' (Lorde,16)

1.2   Retrieve your past

By using the information technology metaphor, we can say that our memory is a system that encodes, stores, and retrieves past experiences.

Encoding means that the information received in your daily life enters your mind as visual, acoustic, and semantic data. Memory functions as a drawer that keeps bits of information, even when you are not aware.

Acoustic memories remind you of sounds, such as music, songs, conversations, familiar voices, sounds of nature. Visual memories make you remember landscapes, photographs, people, places, objects, food, and so forth. Semantic memories remind you of words, sentences, meanings, and concepts. We receive lots of information but it doesn't mean that we store everything. Some data is lost. That's why the process of remembering is sometimes a difficult path.

During the process of storage, the mind selects information by choosing what to store and what to discard. All the knowledge stored in our minds follows a schematic structure in which new data is always connected to old information. Each person has a different way of storing the same experience as it always depends on the way we see the world. According to Neurolinguistics, the study of comprehension, production, and acquisition of language, when people receive the same information, each of us processes it differently because the acquisition of knowledge always depends on previous experiences.

Once our minds go through encoding and storing data, the next step is retrieval. How do we retrieve information? Why is it important for poetry writing? It is the moment of accessing memories, using connections and associations to share experiences. Some memories may not come out easily while others will appear in the form of images, sounds, tastes, feelings, and emotions. For poets, it is crucial to be aware of the way in which the mind processes information we receive every second through our senses as poetry has a lot to do with transposing sensory perception to language. It is more important to reveal how we feel going through some experiences than telling the whole story.

1.3   What is catharsis?

Everybody has reasons to forget some memories. Nobody wants to remember unpleasant and hurtful episodes. Sometimes, forgetting relieves pain. As life must go on, nobody wants to be complaining all the time. A never-ending murmuring hurts the self and bothers people around, nonetheless keeping bad feelings inside causes emotional damage to those who have experienced trauma. The cleansing of painful feelings and memories through writing is called catharsis. Throughout history, poets and novelists have found in cathartic writing a form to relieve the soul, transforming painful memories into poetry. For the poet bell hooks, writing could be a healing place, as she points out, "I worked at explaining the hurt and making it go away." (37)

> Catharsis is a process of releasing strong or repressed emotions. It is a moment of purification of your sadness through art. It is an act of cleansing.

Amnesia is also part of the process of attempting to express traumatic experiences. In poetry writing, amnesia reveals an in-between state of a subject who is at the same time revealing and hiding, covering and uncovering, remembering and forgetting. Forgetting becomes an important element in the creative process as the poetic imagination generally fills the gaps of silence. By combining autobiographical memories with silence, poets find beautiful ways to represent memories.

Poetry is like medicine or therapy thus through poetic lines, we can represent anything. People under situations of terror and suffering, such as periods of dictatorships, migrants, black people under racism, segregation, and so forth, may resort to poetry to represent traumatic experiences.

1.4   Let's read!

After great pain, a formal feeling comes -
  The Nerves sit ceremonious, like Tombs -
   The stiff Heart questions 'was it He, that bore,'
    And 'Yesterday, or Centuries before'?

The Feet, mechanical, go round -
  A Wooden way
   Of Ground, or Air, or Ought -
    Regardless grown,
     A Quartz contentment, like a stone -

This is the Hour of Lead -
  Remembered, if outlived,
   As Freezing persons, recollect the Snow -
    First - Chill - then Stupor - then the letting go -

EMILY DICKINSON, After a great pain (1862)

Pain has an element of blank;
  It cannot recollect
   When it began, or if there was
    A time when it was not.
     It has no future but itself,
      Its infinite realms contain
       Its past, enlightened to perceive
        New periods of pain.

                    EMILY DICKINSON, Pain has an element (1862)

You do not do, you do not do
 Any more, black shoe
  In which I have lived like a foot
   For thirty years, poor and white,
    Barely daring to breathe or Achoo.

Daddy, I have had to kill you.
 You died before I had time -
  Marble-heavy, a bag full of God,
   Ghastly statue with one gray toe
    Big as a Frisco seal

And a head in the freakish Atlantic
 Where it pours bean green over blue
  In the waters off beautiful Nauset.
   I used to pray to recover you.
    Ach, du.

In the German tongue, in the Polish town
 Scraped flat by the roller
  Of wars, wars, wars.

But the name of the town is common.
My Polack friend

Says there are a dozen or two.
So I never could tell where you
Put your foot, your root,
I never could talk to you.
The tongue stuck in my jaw.

It stuck in a barb wire snare.
Ich, ich, ich, ich,
I could hardly speak.
I thought every German was you.
And the language obscene

An engine, an engine
Chuffing me off like a Jew.
A Jew to Dachau, Auschwitz, Belsen.
I began to talk like a Jew.
I think I may well be a Jew.

The snows of the Tyrol, the clear beer of Vienna
Are not very pure or true.
With my gipsy ancestress and my weird luck
And my Taroc pack and my Taroc pack
I may be a bit of a Jew.

I have always been scared of *you*,
With your Luftwaffe, your gobbledygoo.
And your neat mustache
And your Aryan eye, bright blue.
Panzer-man, panzer-man, O You -

Not God but a swastika
  So black no sky could squeak through.
    Every woman adores a Fascist,
      The boot in the face, the brute
        Brute heart of a brute like you.

You stand at the blackboard, daddy,
  In the picture I have of you,
    A cleft in your chin instead of your foot
      But no less a devil for that, no not
        Any less the black man who

Bit my pretty red heart in two.
  I was ten when they buried you.
    At twenty I tried to die
      And get back, back, back to you.
        I thought even the bones would do.

But they pulled me out of the sack,
  And they stuck me together with glue.
    And then I knew what to do.
      I made a model of you,
        A man in black with a Meinkampf look

And a love of the rack and the screw.
  And I said I do, I do.
    So daddy, I'm finally through.
      The black telephone's off at the root,
        The voices just can't worm through.

If I've killed one man, I've killed two -
  The vampire who said he was you

And drank my blood for a year,
  Seven years, if you want to know.
  Daddy, you can lie back now.

There's a stake in your fat black heart
 And the villagers never liked you.
  They are dancing and stamping on you.
  They always *knew* it was you.
   Daddy, daddy, you bastard, I'm through.

SYLVIA PLATH, Daddy (1965)

She is all there.
 She was melted carefully down for you
  and cast up from your childhood,
   cast up from your one hundred favorite aggies.

She has always been there, my darling.
 She is, in fact, exquisite.
  Fireworks in the dull middle of February
  and as real as a cast-iron pot.

Let's face it, I have been momentary.
 A luxury. A bright red sloop in the harbor.
  My hair rising like smoke from the car window.
  Littleneck clams out of season.

She is more than that. She is your have to have,
 has grown you your practical your tropical growth.
  This is not an experiment. She is all harmony.
  She sees to oars and oarlocks for the dinghy,

has placed wild flowers at the window at breakfast,
  sat by the potter's wheel at midday,
    set forth three children under the moon,
      three cherubs drawn by Michelangelo,

done this with her legs spread out
  in the terrible months in the chapel.
    If you glance up, the children are there
      like delicate balloons resting on the ceiling.

She has also carried each one down the hall
  after supper, their heads privately bent,
    two legs protesting, person to person,
      her face flushed with a song and their little sleep.

I give you back your heart.
  I give you permission -

for the fuse inside her, throbbing
  angrily in the dirt, for the bitch in her
    and the burying of her wound -
      for the burying of her small red wound alive -

for the pale flickering flare under her ribs,
  for the drunken sailor who waits in her left pulse,
    for the mother's knee, for the stocking,
      for the garter belt, for the call -

the curious call
  when you will burrow in arms and breasts
    and tug at the orange ribbon in her hair
      and answer the call, the curious call.

She is so naked and singular
She is the sum of yourself and your dream.
Climb her like a monument, step after step.
She is solid.
As for me, I am a watercolor.
I wash off.

ANNE SEXTON, For My Lover, Returning to His Wife (1968)

I remember, I remember,
The house where I was born,
The little window where the sun
Came peeping in at morn;

He never came a wink too soon,
Nor brought too long a day,
But now, I often wish the night
Had borne my breath away!

I remember, I remember,
The roses, red and white,
The vi'lets, and the lily-cups,
Those flowers made of light!
The lilacs where the robin built,
And where my brother set
The laburnum on his birthday, -
The tree is living yet!

I remember, I remember,
Where I was used to swing,
And thought the air must rush as fresh
To swallows on the wing;

My spirit flew in feathers then,
  That is so heavy now,
    And summer pools could hardly cool
    The fever on my brow!

I remember, I remember,
 The fir trees dark and high;
  I used to think their slender tops
   Were close against the sky:
    It was a childish ignorance,
     But now 'tis little joy
      To know I'm farther off from heav'n
      Than when I was a boy.

THOMAS HOOD, I remember I remember (1844)

I've had many an aching pain,
 A for sake o' somebody:
  I have talked, but o' in vain,
   When I thought o' somebody.

Nought could please me any where,
 I could heed nor smile, nor tear;
  And yet I sighed, for half a year!
  And that for sake o' somebody.

She was like the lily fair,
 The rose it blushed, for somebody;
  Her neck was white, her cheek was rare,
   I wot it smiled on somebody; -

Here's good luck to somebody;

And best o' health for somebody;
  The dearest thought I keep mysell,
  I keep for sake o' somebody.

JOHN CLARE, I've had many(1820)

And I remember Spain
  At Easter ripe as an egg for revolt and ruin
  ...
    With writings on the walls
    Hammer and sickle, Boicot, Viva, Muera;

      ...
      With shadows of the poor,
        The begging cripples and the children begging
        ...
          With powerful or banal
            Monuments of riches or repression
            And the Escorial
            Cold for ever within like the heart of Philip.
            ...
              With slovenly soldiers, nuns,
                And peeling posters from the last elections
                Promising bread or guns
                ...
                  And Avila was cold
                    And Segovia was picturesque and smelly
                    ...
                      And we sat in trains all night
                        With the windows shut among civil guards and
peasants

...

And the next day took the boat
For home, forgetting Spain.

LOUIS MACNEICE, And I remember Spain (1938)

I love it, I love it; and who shall dare
 To chide me for loving that old arm-chair?
  I've treasured it long as a sainted prize,
   I've bedew'd it with tears, and embalmed it with sighs;
    'Tis bound by a thousand bands to my heart;
    Not a tie will break, not a link will start.
     Would ye learn the spell? a mother sat there,
     And a sacred thing is that old arm-chair.

In childhood's hour I linger'd near
 The hallow'd seat with list'ning ear;
  And gentle words that mother would give,
   To fit me to die and teach me to live.
    She told me shame would never betide,
     With truth for my creed and God for my guide;
      She taught me to lisp my earliest prayer,
       As I knelt beside that old arm-chair.

I sat and watch'd her many a day,
 When her eye grew dim, and her locks were grey;
  And I almost worshipp'd her when she smil'd
  And turn'd from her Bible to bless her child.
    Years roll'd on, but the last one sped -
     My idol was shatter'd, my earth-star fled;
      I learnt how much the heart can bear,
       When I saw her die in that old arm-chair.
        'Tis past! 'tis past! but I gaze on it now

With quivering breath and throbbing brow:
 'Twas there she nursed me, 'twas there she died;
 And memory flows with lava tide.
  Say it is folly, and deem me weak,
   While the scalding drops start down my cheek;
   But I love it, I love it, and cannot tear
   My soul from a mother's old arm-chair.

ELIZA COOK, The Old Arm Chair (1856)

You may write me down in history
 With your bitter, twisted lies,
  You may trod me in the very dirt
   But still, like dust, I'll rise.

Does my sassiness upset you?
 Why are you beset with gloom?
  'Cause I walk like I've got oil wells
   Pumping in my living room.

Just like moons and like suns,
 With the certainty of tides,
  Just like hopes springing high,
   Still I'll rise.

Did you want to see me broken?
 Bowed head and lowered eyes?
  Shoulders falling down like teardrops,
   Weakened by my soulful cries?

Does my haughtiness offend you?
 Don't you take it awful hard
  'Cause I laugh like I've got gold mines
   Diggin' in my own backyard.

You may shoot me with your words,
 You may cut me with your eyes,
  You may kill me with your hatefulness,
   But still, like air, I'll rise.

Does my sexiness upset you?
 Does it come as a surprise
  That I dance like I've got diamonds
   At the meeting of my thighs?

Out of the huts of history's shame
 I rise
  Up from a past that's rooted in pain
   I rise
    I'm a black ocean, leaping and wide,
     Welling and swelling I bear in the tide.

Leaving behind nights of terror and fear
 I rise
  Into a daybreak that's wondrously clear
   I rise
    Bringing the gifts that my ancestors gave,
     I am the dream and the hope of the slave.
      I rise
       I rise
        I rise.

MAYA ANGELOU, Still I Rise' (1978)

1.5   Snapshot

By combining memories with imagination, Emily Dickinson, Sylvia Plath, Anne Sexton, Thomas Hood, Eliza Cook, and Maya Angelou teach us how to focus on the past to write poetry.

In Emily Dickinson's poems, the speaker hides painful memories, revealing trauma and bringing to light the pain as the main element of these two poems. Dickinson describes the impossibility to deal with memories that remain in the darkness of the mind, and, as we read in the first line of the poem, "After a great pain, a formal feeling comes," we understand how the words chill, stupor, freeze, mechanical feet reveal deep suffering able to paralyze everything around. She is a person who responds as a machine without realizing that the world didn't stop.

The verb "remember" connected to "survival" deals with the ambivalence of carrying on life instead of living. By turning her pain into the main theme of this poem, the poet doesn't reveal any memories, but her need to exorcise sadness as the pain haunts the self, throwing her into darkness. Writing about this pain means an attempt to let it go.

In the second poem, Pain has Element of Blank, Dickinson represents the silence of a mind that resists remembering. "It cannot recollect," she says. The poet describes someone who speaks from a chasm, a person who cannot recollect some experiences. Time is a spiral as the painful experience determines new periods of pain in the present and the future. Enjambment gradually discloses verse after verse the ambivalent state of someone who tries to go through a process of catharsis.

In Daddy, Sylvia Plath brings to light memories of her father. The relation between a poem and the poet's personal experiences may be very delicate but many times we found a correlation between life and poetry. This poem resonates with some aspects of Plath's personal life as she had a German father who worked as a Professor at a respectable university and died when she was eight years old. Plath tried to commit suicide a couple of times before ending her life at the age of 36. By revealing her father as a brute who had a swastika on the wall, "Not God but a swastika/ So black no sky could squeak through," Plath confesses that as a child she feared him "I have always been scared of you."

Sylvia Plath's poem becomes an instrument to exorcise not only sadness and bitterness but also the shame of the father. It is a deep shame that gives birth to the process of catharsis. From a feminist perspective, the poet draws an invisible frontier between imagination and her childhood memories to express feelings of sadness, embarrassment, and disrespect. Poetry gave her tools to reject the father in the verses of Daddy, and she says, "Daddy, I have had to kill you./ You died before I had time." In many ways, we observe how the metaphorical erasure of this hurtful memory turns into an attempt to relieve her soul.

Anne Sexton's poem describes the life of a woman who has been a mother or a wife, dedicated to the family while her own life vanishes. The woman represented here does not see her own life as meaningful. Anne Sexton's poem has some ambiguities as she describes the woman as a solid, strong woman who is ready to take care of her children who are always well educated and polite. She is the perfect wife, but she ceases to exist. She carries everything in the house but she buries her wounds or her sadness, her frustration. The poem has some concepts of first-wave feminism that rejected the idea of domesticity as the main role of women in the patriarchal society.

In Still I Rise, Maya Angelou points out how historical narratives manipulate black people's experiences. In the lines 'you may write me down in history/ With your bitter, twisted lies,' the poem reveals how history, 'gives contradictory signals about the value of remembering in the much longer span of collective history.'(Sontag,115) In many ways, forgetting turns into the best way to make peace and to reconcile but Angelou's poem reminds us that remembering is crucial to moving forward.

By bringing to light hurtful collective memories, Angelou's poem deals with the resilience and resistance of a black woman who has come to terms with the consequences of racism and segregation in America. Inscribed in the womanist and black feminist tradition, Maya Angelou's writing aims to provide more than a personal catharsis, her poem becomes a collective voice for black women who need to rise despite the multiple barriers.

1.6   Practice

It's your turn

Read carefully the poems in this section. Take a few minutes to think about some memories that have deeply changed you. Choose a moment in your life and describe it in a few lines. Be honest. Use your memories and your imagination. You can use some ambivalence and images to describe how you feel. You can try short poems as Dickinson's The Pain or long ones as Plath's Daddy and Sexton's For My Lover, Returning to His Wife. You can also get inspired by Maya Angelou Still I Rise and tell a story about resilience. It is important to do this exercise before going to the next section.

1.7   Poets

Emily Dickinson (1830 - 1886)

was born in Amherst, Massachusetts, and spent nearly all her life within its confines. She rarely left her house. Only seven of her 1.775 poems were published in her lifetime. Not until 1890, four years after her death, did a selection of her poems appeared in print.

Sylvia Plath (1932 - 1963)

was born in Boston. Her father, who taught German at Boston University, died in 1940 when she was eight years old. She won a fellowship to attend Cambridge University in England and married the English poet Red Hughes in 1956. She separated from her husband in 1962 and committed suicide in 1963.

Anne Sexton (1928 - 1974)

was born Anne Gray Harvey in Newton, Massachusets. When she was twenty, she had a psychotic breakdown and attempted suicide. Sexton studied with Robert Lowell and participated in the "confessional" poetry project established by him and W. D. Snodgrass. She was found dead inside an idling car parked in a garage on 4 October 1974.

Thomas Hood (1799 - 1845)

was a journalist, humorist and poetic crusader for the poor. He was born in Poultry in the city of London. He turned to journalism in 1921, working as a sub-director on the London Magazine. He lost all his assets in 1834. In 1844, he broke down completely leaving him as his wife destitute. He died 3 May 1845.

John Clare (1793 - 1864)

was born in Helton, Northamptonshire. He worked at sev-

eral casual and seasonal rural jobs. He married Martha
Turner and they had eight children. In the mid-thirty he
was suffering memory loss and delusions. In December
1841 he was certified insane and put in the new St An-
drew's County Lunatic Asylum, and there he stayed until
his death in 20 May 1864.

Eliza Cook (1818 - 1889)

was born in Southwark, the youngest of eleven children of
the metal trader Joseph Cook. Her best-known poem is
"The Old Arm-Chair" was published when she was eigh-
teen. She started up her own monthly journal in 1849, a
periodical written by herself with a feminist flavor on the
subjects of marriage, clothing education and so forth. She
never married, and rumors of lesbianism clustered about
her name. She died at Wimbledon, 28 September 1889.

Maya Angelou (1928 - 2014)

was an American poet, memoirist, and civil rights, ac-
tivist. She published seven books of essays and several
books of poetry and autobiographies. She received dozens
of awards and more than 50 honorary degrees. She was an
actor, writer, director, and producer of plays, movies, and
public television shows. In 1982, she was named the first
Reynolds Professor of American Studies. She was active
in the Civil Rights Movement. She worked with Martin
Luther King and Malcom X. In 1993, Angelou recited a
poem at the first inauguration of Bill Clinton. She was
awarded the Presidential Medal of Freedom by Barack
Obama in 2011.

LOUIS MACNEICE 1907- 1963

Born in Belfast Frederick Louis MacNeice was an outsider
almost from the beginning. MacNeice was raised among
books and began writing poetry at the age of seven. By
the time he went up to Merton College at Oxford in 1926,

his reading included such modern poets as Edith Sitwell and T. S. Eliot.

References

Lorde, Audre. 'Poetry is not a Luxury' in Feminist Theory edited by Wendy Kolmar and Frances Bartkowski. McGraw Hill: New York, 2005.

hooks, bell. 'Theory as Liberatory Practice' in Feminist Theory edited by Wendy Kolmar and Frances Bartkowski. McGraw Hill: New York, 2005.

Sontag, Susan. Regarding the Pain of the Others. Picador: New York, 2003.

Chapter 2

EKPHRASIS

> "... poetry as a method to achieve clairvoyance, of
> obtaining the knowledge we need to move
> forward,..."

> Robin Kelley, "A Poetics of Anticolonialism"

ALL this talk about imagination, forgetting, and cathar-
sis brings us back to an important area called inspira-
tion. Where does inspiration come from? Do all poems come
from personal experiences? This chapter focuses on how vi-
sual works of art can inspire someone to write poetry. Did you
know that a paint or a scuplture can be a source of inspiration?

Ekphrasis is a written description, an interpretation, or
a rhetorical commentary of a visual work of art.

An ekphrastic poem is an aesthetic response in which poets
unveil how the pleasure caused by the arts provokes a reflective
analysis. As poets write about a painting, they try to find
concealed meanings as well as add new meanings to the work
of art.

2.1   Aesthetics

Aesthetics comes from the Greek aesthesis that refers to the appreciation of beauty. The aesthetic response involves a multitude of experiences, from visual to emotional, and self-reflection. Works of art transform the viewer in multiple ways, producing a spiritual experience beyond consciousness and embodiment.

This transcendental nature of art functions as a religion, and can alleviate the mind and soul or disconnect one from everyday problems and difficulties. Its intrinsic power makes people imagine new realities and dream of a better world. This connection with the inner self is crucial and necessary as people contact the invisible and the spiritual in the human search of the divine.

While beauty might seem a usual concept for most of us, the philosopher Immanuel Kant introduced the concept of the Sublime in the arts.

For Kant, beautiful art meant a work excelling in grace and form that delights the eye, providing the viewer with an aesthetic experience and incomprehensible emotion.

An ekphrastic work is the poet's attempt to describe the Sublime or the beauty of a visual work of art.

2.2   Let's read!

About suffering they were never wrong,
The old Masters: how well they understood

Its human position: how it takes place
 While someone else is eating or opening a window or just
  walking dully along;
   How, when the aged are reverently, passionately waiting
    For the miraculous birth, there always must be
     Children who did not specially want it to happen,skating
      On a pond at the edge of the wood:
       They never forgot
        That even the dreadful martyrdom must run its course
         Anyhow in a corner, some untidy spot
          Where the dogs go on with their doggy life and the
           Torturer's horse
            Scratches its innocent behind on a tree.

In Breughel's Icarus, for instance: how everything turns away
 Quite leisurely from the disaster; the ploughman may
  Have heard the splash, the forsaken cry,
   But for him it was not an important failure; the sun shone
    As it had to on the white legs disappearing into the green
     Water,and the expensive delicate ship that must have seen
      Something amazing, a boy falling out of the sky,
       Had somewhere to get to and sailed calmly on.

W. H. AUDEN, Musee des Beaux Arts (1939)

According to Brueghel
 when Icarus fell
  it was spring

a farmer was ploughing
 his field
  the whole pageantry

of the year was
  awake tingling
    near

the edge of the sea
  concerned
    with itself

sweating in the sun
  that melted
    the wings' wax

unsignificantly
  off the coast
    there was

a splash quite unnoticed
  this was
    Icarus drowning

WILLIAM CARLOS WILLIAMS, Landscape with the Fall of Icarus
(1960)

Heading to the city,
  White buildings he saw
   But blinded by the sun,
    His wings he lost.
     In a village he fell;
       Villagers did not care
         For what happened to Icarus.
           His destiny meant nothing as
             Life continued, the traveler passed by,

The plowman kept his working,
The fisherman continued his daily catch.
His wings,
Other men borrowed
To fly away to the city
He could never see.
But in the deep ocean,
Icarus saw other corpses
Of dreamers like him.

MARY BISHOP, Brueghel's Icarus (1988)

The over-all picture is winter
icy mountains
in the background the return

from the hunt it is toward evening
from the left
sturdy hunters lead in

their pack the inn-sign
hanging from a
broken hinge is a stag a crucifix

between his antlers the cold
inn yard is
deserted but for a huge bonfire

that flares wind-driven tended by
women who cluster
about it to the right beyond

the hill is a pattern of skaters
 Brueghel the painter
  concerned with it all has chosen

a winter-struck bush for his
 foreground to
  complete the picture

WILLIAM CARLOS WILLIAMS, The Hunters in the Snow (1960)

Historic, side-long, implicating eyes;
 A smile of velvet's lustre on the cheek;
  Calm lips the smile leads upward; hand that lies
   Glowing and soft, the patience in its rest
    Of cruelty that waits and does not seek
     For prey; a dusky forehead and a breast
      Where twilight touches ripeness amorously:
       Behind her, crystal rocks, a sea and skies
        Of evanescent blue on cloud and creek;
         Landscape that shines suppressive of its zest
          For those vicissitudes by which men die.

MICHAEL FIELD, La Gioconda Leonardo da Vinci, The Louvre (1892)

'Tis Leda lovely, wild and free,
 Drawing her gracious Swan down through the grass to see
  Certain round eggs without a speck:
   One hand plunged in the reeds and dinting the downy neck,

Although his hectoring bill
 Gapes toward her tresses,

She draws the fondled creature to her will.
She joys to bend in the live light
Her glistening body toward her love, how much more bright!
  Though on her breast the sunshine lies
    And spreads its affluence on the wide curves of her waist and thighs,
To her meek, smitten gaze
Where her hand presses
  The Swan's white neck sink Heaven's concentred rays.

MICHAEL FIELD, A Pen-Drawing of Leda(1892)

VENUS is sad among the wanton powers,
That make delicious tempest in the hours
Of April or are reckless with their flowers:
Through umbrageous orange-trees
Sweeps, mid azure swirl, the Breeze,
That with clipping arms would seize
Eôs, wind-inspired and mad,
In wind-tightened muslin clad,
With one tress for stormy wreath
And a bine between her teeth.
Flora foots it near in frilled,
Vagrant skirt, with roses filled;
Pinks and gentians spot her robe
And the curled acanthus-lobe
Edges intricate her sleeve;
Rosy briars a girdle weave,
Blooms are brooches in her hair:
Though a vision debonair,
Thriftless, venturesome, a grace
Disingenuous lights her face;
Curst she is, uncertain-lipped,
Riggishly her dress is whipped
By little gusts fantastic. Will she deign

To toss her double-roses, or refrain?

These riot by the left side of the queen;
Before her face another group is seen:
In ordered and harmonic nobleness,
Three maidens circle o'er the turf—each dress
Blown round the tiptoe shape in lovely folds
Of air-invaded white; one comrade holds
Her fellow's hand on high, the foremost links
Their other hands in chain that lifts and sinks.
Their auburn tresses ripple, coil or sweep;
Gems, amulets and fine ball-fringes keep
Their raiment from austereness. With reserve
The dancers in a garland slowly curve.
They are the Graces in their virgin youth;
And does it touch their Deity with ruth
That they must fade when Eros speeds his dart?
Is this the grief and forethought of her heart?

For she is sad, although fresh myrtles near
Her figure chequer with their leaves the drear,
Grey chinks that through the orange-trees appear:
Clothed in spring-time's white and red,
She is tender with some dread,
As she turns a musing head
Sideways mid her veil demure;
Her wide eyes have no allure,
Dark and heavy with their pain.
She would bless, and yet in vain
Is her troubled blessing : Love,
Blind and tyrannous above,
Shoots his childish flame to mar
Those without defect, who are
Yet unspent and cold with peace;

While, her sorrow to increase,
Hermes, leader of her troop—
His short cutlass on the loop
Of a crimson cloak, his eye
Clear in its fatality—
Rather seems the guide of ghosts
To the dead, Plutonian coasts,
Than herald of Spring's immature, gay band:
He plucks a ripened orange with his hand.

The tumult and the mystery of earth,
When woods are bleak and flowers have sudden birth,
When love is cruel, follow to their end
The God that teaches Shadows to descend,
But pauses now awhile, with solemn lip
And left hand laid victorious on his hip.
The triumph of the year without avail
Is blown to Hades by blue Zephyr's gale.
Across the seedling herbage coltsfoot grows
Between the tulip, heartsease, strawberry-rose,
Fringed pinks and dull grape-hyacinth. Alas,
At play together, through the speckled grass
Trip Youth and April : Venus, looking on,
Beholds the mead with all the dancers gone.

MICHAEL FIELD, Spring Sandro Botticelli (1892)

2.3 Snapshot

William Carlos William and W.H. Auden's ekphrastic po-
ems inspired by Brueghel's painting The Fall of Icarus let us
know that the "Old Masters," as Auden refers to Brueghel,
knew how to represent the human condition. Auden high-

lights life that goes on despite the pain someone inflicts on the other, as he says, 'Where the dogs go on with their doggy life and the torturer's horse/Scratches its innocent behind on a tree.' Brueghel depicts people who do not give much attention to what is happening in front of their eyes.

For Auden and Williams, the viewer is positioned as one of Brueghel's characters, and, like the plowman or the fisherman, we hardly see Icarus' legs disappearing into the sea. Both poems focus on the insignificance of Icarus' fall for those who decided to carry on their lives. As the painter conceals Icarus and plays with the way we experience reality, we ask questions that lead us to look at ourselves, "What's going on?" "Why couldn't I perceive this?" or "What matters to us?"

Auden and Williams' ekphrastic poems remind us of Michel Foucault's essay on Diego Velazquez's painting. In his book entitled The Order of Things, published in 1966, Foucault begins with a lengthy discussion of Las Meninas, arguing that, in his famous painting, Velazquez uses light to play with a complex gaze, concealing the most important subject of the painting.

Thus, the painting represents conflicting viewpoints on the relationship between art and reality that involves how we see reality. In 'Las Meninas,' the presence of the artist or the looking glass, in which we see a reflection of the King and the Queen, makes the observer think of what is central and what is at the margins.

For Foucault, Velazquez reverses the subject/object positions, destabilizing the subject who loses his fixity. By dislocating the subject, Foucault questions the very idea of truth and reality.

Auden and William's ekphrastic poems also question the idea of what matters in the painting as Brueghel reinvents the myth of Icarus, dislocating the subject and disturbing our gaze. By describing how Brueghel's characters do not care about Icarus, the poems not only reflect on the vulnerability of Icarus, they come to terms with the notion of truth and how we perceive reality.

2.4   Practice

It's your turn

Read carefully the poems in this section. Go to a museum or search some visual works on internet. Some painters you can look for: Van Gogh, Rembrandt, Botticelli, Monet, Velazquez, Brueghel. Write two poems.

2.5   Poets

Wynstan Hugh Auden (1907 - 1973)
was born in York, England and moved to New York in 1939. He studied at Oxford University where he participated in a literary circle which included Stephen Spender, Christopher Isherwood and C. Day Lewis. He became an American citizen in 1946. He wrote brilliant essays, enduring poems, and was also anthologist an editor.

Williams Carlos Williams (1883 - 1963)
was born in Rutherford, New Jersey. He is known as the greatest modern master of free verse. He studied medicine at the University of Pennsylvania, set up a private practice in Rutherford, and became chief of pediatrics at the General Hospital in Paterson, New Jersey. He won the Pulitzer prize in 1962 with the work Pictures from Brueghel.

Michael Field (1864-1914)

was the collaborative writing name of Katherine Bradley and her niece Emma Cooper. In 1878, the pair attended class together in Bristol where the family had moved from Kenilworth. In Bristol, they argued for votes for women in the college debating society. Michael Field came into being with the work Calirrhoe and Fair Rosamund (1884) and from then on remained their public name. They were familiar figures on London's aestheticist and symbolist fringe.

References

Kelley, Robin. 'A Poetics of Anticolonialism,' in Aimé Discourse on Colonialism, translate Monthly Review Press: New York, 1972.

Hooks, bell. 'Theory as Liberatory Practice' in Feminist Theory edited by Wendy Kolmar and Frances Bartkowski. McGraw Hill: New York, 2005.

Chapter 3

QUOTIDIAN AND POETRY

What presides over the poem is not the most lucid
intelligence, the sharpest sensibility or the subtlest
feelings, but experience as a whole.

Aimé Césaire, Poetry and Knowledge

THIS This chapter focuses on how to write poetry about the
commonplace, plain, and simple episodes and things of
everyday life. Quotidian has to do with a phone conversation,
a person you see every day at the same place, a bench in the
park, an old chair, an old book, anything. You may ask "How
can someone write a poem about an object?" "Is it possible
to see something unusual and uncommon within the usual and
familiar?" "Can you see something special in the simple things
of everyday life?"

Poets usually attempt to see the essence of usual things. It
is called phenomenology. Now you need to understand what
it means.

3.1   Phenomenology

A phenomenon is a fact or a situation, an occurrence, event, episode, a sight, a thing, a daily experience. The term came into usage through the philosopher Immanuel Kant (1724-1804) who defined a phenomenon as any object apprehended by the senses. Through the senses, we learn from experiences, naming the objects we observe, for example, a house, a book, a pen, and so forth. As we tend to focus on the appearance of things, making conclusions based on what we see, we don't take time to think about the nature of things. You must be asking, 'How could I see the essence of things?

Phenomenology, a branch of philosophy developed by the philosopher Edmund Husserl (1874-1928), means the reflective analysis of experiences of life. The idea is to reveal what is behind the appearance or the essence of human experiences in events of everyday life. The essence we look for as we observe life is already deep inside of us, and as the poet Aimé Césaire points out,

> ... every history, every future, every dream, every life form, from plant to animal, every creative impulse – is plumbed from the depths of the unconscious.

Inspired by a sense of wonder, like philosophers, poets should ask questions about things and situations, 'Why is this old chair special?' 'Can I write a poem about a chair?' 'What does it represent?' 'How long has it been here?' In this sense, every single object, place, or situation can become a source of inspiration.

Writing poetry means the possibility of approaching an event or an object from a different perspective, and poets may decide to go for a walk to write about simple things of life. It is like Plato's allegory of the dark cave.

In the allegory, Plato tells the story of Socrates who was one of the prisoners in the cave but manages to escape. Socrates and other prisoners are chained in the cave, tied to their sits and cannot move. There is a light coming from a fire right behind them, and they can only see shadows projected on the wall in front of them.

After a while, they believe that the shadows are the real world. When Socrates gets free from the chains and escapes, he comes back to the cave to tell the prisoners that they only see shadows. At the end of the story, the prisoners kill the philosopher and keep looking at the shadows.

Handcuffed by preconceived ideas about life, some people end up like those prisoners who lost their sense of wonder and curiosity. Getting free from this cave means questioning what seems true and commonplace.

3.2   Everyday life and haiku

A haiku is a poetic form that describes a situation of everyday life. Haiku is an unrhymed very short poem that has seventeen syllables, arranged in three lines, with the formation 5-7-5. The second line must have seven syllables, the first and third ones, five syllables. It comes from the Japanese literature, and the word derived from hokku, the first three verses of a long poetic form called renga. The hokku gives a general description of a renga, featuring themes as a season, moment of the day, landscape. People loved hokku so much that in the late 19th century, the hokku renamed haiku, became an independent form.

> Always in the present tense, a traditional haiku captures a moment with objectivity without many details or subjective interpretation.

The haiku should have a Kigo and a Kireji. A Kigo is a word that refers to the natural world, for instance, seasons, flowers, trees, and a Kireji is a pause that appears in the end of the second line. A haiku often has an image in each of the three verses.

In English, haiku may vary. The use of Kigo may appear as metaphors and similes and the use of Kireji can appear in the form of colon, dash, semicolon, ellipsis, giving the idea of movement and separating the haiku into two parts that complement each other. However, poets usually experiment with haiku, adapting the form to the message they want to express, as we observe in Sonia Sanchez and Ezra Pound's poems,

Example: English haiku
Picture this woman
of royalty...wearing a crown
of morning air...

SONIA SANCHEZ, Haiku for Harriet Tubman

Example: English haiku
The apparition of these faces in the crowd;
Petals on a wet, black bough.

EZRA POUND, In a Station of the Metro (1913)

3.3 Let's read!

The pool players. Seven at the golden shovel.

We real cool. We
 Left school. We

Lurk late. We
 Strike straight. We

Sing sin. We
 Thin gin. We

Jazz June. We
 Die soon

GWENDOLYN BROOKS, We Real Cool (1960)

With fingers weary and worn,
 With eyelids heavy and red,
  A woman sat in unwomanly rags,
   Plying her needle and thread—
    Stitch! stitch! stitch!
     In poverty, hunger, and dirt,
      And still with a voice of dolorous pitch
       She sang the "Song of the Shirt."

"Work! work! work!
 While the cock is crowing aloof!
  And work—work—work,
   Till the stars shine through the roof!
    It's O! to be a slave

Along with the barbarous Turk,
    Where woman has never a soul to save,
    If this is Christian work!

"Work—work—work,
  Till the brain begins to swim;
  Work—work—work,
    Till the eyes are heavy and dim!
    Seam, and gusset, and band,
      Band, and gusset, and seam,
        Till over the buttons I fall asleep,
        And sew them on in a dream!

"O, men, with sisters dear!
  O, men, with mothers and wives!
  It is not linen you're wearing out,
    But human creatures' lives!
    Stitch—stitch—stitch,
      In poverty, hunger and dirt,
        Sewing at once, with a double thread,
        A Shroud as well as a Shirt.

"But why do I talk of death?
  That phantom of grisly bone,
  I hardly fear his terrible shape,
    It seems so like my own—
    t seems so like my own,
      Because of the fasts I keep;
        Oh, God! that bread should be so dear.
        And flesh and blood so cheap!

"Work—work—work!
  My labour never flags;
  And what are its wages? A bed of straw,

A crust of bread—and rags.
  That shattered roof—this naked floor—
  A table—a broken chair—
    And a wall so blank, my shadow I thank
    For sometimes falling there!

"Work—work—work!
 From weary chime to chime,
  Work—work—work,
    As prisoners work for crime!
    Band, and gusset, and seam,
      Seam, and gusset, and band,
        Till the heart is sick, and the brain benumbed,
        As well as the weary hand.

"Work—work—work,
 In the dull December light,
  And work—work—work,
    When the weather is warm and bright—
    While underneath the eaves
      The brooding swallows cling
        As if to show me their sunny backs
        And twit me with the spring.

"O! but to breathe the breath
 Of the cowslip and primrose sweet—
  With the sky above my head,
    And the grass beneath my feet;
      For only one short hour
        To feel as I used to feel,
          Before I knew the woes of want
          And the walk that costs a meal!

"O! but for one short hour!
 A respite however brief!
  No blessed leisure for Love or hope,
   But only time for grief!
    A little weeping would ease my heart,
     But in their briny bed
      My tears must stop, for every drop
      Hinders needle and thread!"

With fingers weary and worn,
 With eyelids heavy and red,
  A woman sat in unwomanly rags,
   Plying her needle and thread—
    Stitch! stitch! stitch!
     In poverty, hunger, and dirt,
      And still with a voice of dolorous pitch,—
       Would that its tone could reach the Rich!—
       She sang this "Song of the Shirt!"

THOMAS HOOD, The song of the shirt (1843)

When men were all asleep the snow came flying,
In large white flakes falling on the city brown,
Stealthily and perpetually settling and loosely lying,
Hushing the latest traffic of the drowsy town;
Deadening, muffling, stifling its murmurs failing;
Lazily and incessantly floating down and down:
Silently sifting and veiling road, roof and railing;
Hiding difference, making unevenness even,
Into angles and crevices softly drifting and sailing.
All night it fell, and when full inches seven
It lay in the depth of its uncompacted lightness,
The clouds blew off from a high and frosty heaven;

And all woke earlier for the unaccustomed brightness
Of the winter dawning, the strange unheavenly glare:
The eye marvelled—marvelled at the dazzling whiteness;
The ear hearkened to the stillness of the solemn air;
No sound of wheel rumbling nor of foot falling,
And the busy morning cries came thin and spare.
Then boys I heard, as they went to school, calling,
They gathered up the crystal manna to freeze
Their tongues with tasting, their hands with snowballing;
Or rioted in a drift, plunging up to the knees;
Or peering up from under the white-mossed wonder,
'O look at the trees!' they cried, 'O look at the trees!'
With lessened load a few carts creak and blunder,
Following along the white deserted way,
A country company long dispersed asunder:
When now already the sun, in pale display
Standing by Paul's high dome, spread forth below
His sparkling beams, and awoke the stir of the day.
For now doors open, and war is waged with the snow;
And trains of sombre men, past tale of number,
Tread long brown paths, as toward their toil they go:
But even for them awhile no cares encumber
Their minds diverted; the daily word is unspoken,
The daily thoughts of labour and sorrow slumber
At the sight of the beauty that greets them, for the charm they
have broken.

ROBERT BRIDGES, London Snow (1890)

An omnibus across the bridge
Crawls like a yellow butterfly,
And, here and there a passer-by
Shows like a little restless midge.

Big barges full of yellow hay
 Are moored against the shadowy wharf,
  And, like a yellow silken scarf,
   The thick fog hangs along the quay.

The yellow leaves begin to fade
 And flutter from the temple elms,
  And at my feet the pale green Thames
   Lies like a rod of rippled jade.

OSCAR WILDE, Symphony in Yellow (1889)

 so much depends
  upon

a red wheel
 barrow

glazed with rain
 water

beside the white
 chickens

WILLIAM CARLOS WILLIAMS, The Red Wheelbarrow (1923)

I have eaten
 the plums
  that were in
   the icebox

and which
 you were probably
  saving
   for breakfast

Forgive me
 they were delicious
  so sweet
   and so cold

WILLIAM CARLOS WILLIAMS, This is just to say (1934)

In the south, sleeping against
 the drugstore, growling under
  the trucks and stoves, stumbling
   through and over the cluttered eyes
    of early mysterious night. Frowning
     drunk waving moving a hand or lash.
      Dancing kneeling reaching out, letting
       a hand rest in shadows. Squatting
        to drink or pee. Stretching to climb
         pulling themselves onto horses near
          where there was sea (the old songs
           lead you to believe). Riding out
            from this town, to another, where
             it is also black. Down a road
              where people are asleep. Towards

the moon or the shadows of houses.
Towards the songs' pretended sea.

AMIRI BARAKA, Legacy (1969)

The chatter of little people
 Breaks on my purpose
  Like the water-drops which slowly wear the rocks to powder.
  And while I laugh
   My spirit crumbles at their teasing touch.

AMY LOWELL, Aliens (1955)

All day I have watched the purple vine leaves
 Fall into the water.
  And now in the moonlight they still fall,
   But each leaf is fringed with silver.

AMY LOWELL, Autumn (1955)

There are so many roots to the tree of anger
 that sometimes the branches shatter
  before they bear.
   Sitting in Nedicks
    the women rally before they march
     discussing the problematic girls
      they hire to make them free.
       An almost white counterman passes
        a waiting brother to serve them first
         and the ladies neither notice nor reject
          the slighter pleasures of their slavery.
           But I who am bound by my mirror
            as well as my bed

Sell your books at World of Books!
Go to sell.worldofbooks.com and get an instant price quote. We even pay the shipping - see what your old books are worth today!

Inspected By: rudy_sacrab

00091128195

see causes in colour
as well as sex
and sit here wondering
which me will survive

AUDRE LORDE, Who said it was simple (1973)

3.4 Snapshot

In the poem "A Station of the Metro", Ezra Pound does not use any verb, only fourteen words. He paints an image not only to make us see what he sees but to make us feel the way he felt. As one of the founders of a literary movement called Imagism, the poet relied on linguistic economy and objectivity to emphasize the central role of the experience.

The poem focuses on everyday life, contrasting it to the natural world. In his two verses, Pound used a few words to depict an image in a metro station in Paris. First, he makes the reader see the crowd in the station. The word apparition in the first verse, meaning ghostly, gives an idea of something disconnected from the real world or non-human. In the second verse, he uses a metaphor to compare the crowd to petals, hanging on a branch, referring to the crowd's fragility as petals, while the black bough gives us the contrasting image of darkness and coldness. Here, we can see a crowd in the darkness and isolation of the metro looking like petals hanging on a cold branch. And what do we feel? We feel non-humans. We feel fragile and isolated in the crowd.

Gwendolyn Brooks' poem is also about everyday life. In an interview, Brooks said that she was walking home, saw a group of seven boys playing during school time. The rhythm is one of the most important features in this poem. It makes the reader feels how life goes faster without the boys perceiving that it is ephemeral. The jazz rhythm contrasts with the mourning tone at the end of the poem. The verb die in the last verse marks the end of the movement, contrasting with jazz, sing, strike. Brooks' poem calls attention to social problems as exclusion, poverty, and marginalization, and lack of education that target vulnerable communities in the U.S.

Brooks does not say explicitly how the education system contributes to school avoidance by black children who have to come to terms with bullying, racial discrimination, or anxiety by being neglected by teachers. In some school communities, education hasn't been taken seriously, and children do not have reasons to feel enthusiastic about school. Gwendolyn Brooks' poem gives us space to reflect on social issues and the role of education. On one side, a poor education system pushes vulnerable children out of school, on the other, lack of education is one of the reasons for poverty and exclusion.

3.5   Practice

It's your turn

Now, it is your turn. Go for a walk, observe a phenomenon, an occurrence, a situation, a thing, anything in your everyday life, and write a few poems about it. Don't forget to count the words, organize your poem in three lines, and use the kigo and the kireji.

3.6   Poets

Ezra Pound (1885-1972)

was born in Hailey, Idaho and was considered the most controversial figure in modern poetry. He translated po-

etry from Greek, Latin, Anglo-Saxon and Chinese, caus-
ing a rethinking of what it was possible to do in verse
translation and in poetry in general.

Gwendolyn Brooks (1917-2000)

was born in Topeka, Kansas, and grew up in Chicago's
South Side. Her first poem appeared in print when she
was thirteen. She received encouragement from Langston
Hughes. She wrote about the condition of black people in
Chicago, including themes as poverty and racial prejudice.
In 1950, she became the first African American poet to
win the Pulitzer Prize.

Robert Bridges (1844-1930)

was born in Kent into a prosperous land-owning fam-
ily. He was the fourth son and eighth child of Thomas
Bridges and Harriet Affleck. He produced his first volume
of Poem and graduated in Medicine in 1874. He practiced
medicine London hospitals, living with his mother in Bed-
ford Square. In 1884, he married Monica Waterhouse and
had three children. He was chosen as a Poet Laureate in
1913.

Oscar Wilde (1854-1900)

was born in Dublin, middle child of Dr. William Wilde,
an ear-eye surgeon and Jane Francesca Elgee, archdea-
con's granddaughter, translator, poet of the nationalist
Young Ireland movement of the forties. Wilde was sent
to the Protestant Portora Royal School in Enniskillen in
the Protestant north of Ireland, and then to Trinity Col-
lege, Dublin. He graduated in Classics in 1874. He went
on a scholarship to study Classics at Magdalen College,
Oxford, 1874-5. He travelled widely, lecturing in North
America in 1882. He married Constance Lloyd, had two
sons and settled in Chelsea. His great literary days began
with the publication of The Happy Prince stories (1888),

and in 1889 The Picture of Dorian Gray first appeared in Lippincott's Monthly Magazine (1890).

Sonia Sanchez (1934-)

is an American poet, writer, and professor. She was a leading figure in the Black Arts Movement and has written over a dozen books of poetry, as well as short stories, critical essays, plays, and children's books. In the 1960s, Sanchez released poems in periodicals targeted towards African-American audience and published her debut collection, Homecoming, in 1969. In 1993, she receive the Pew Fellowship of Arts.

References

Cesáire, Aimé. 'Poetry and Knowledge' in Refusal of Shadow: Surrealism and the Caribbean, trans. by Michael Richardson and Krzysztof Fijalkowski, London:Verso, 1996.

Chapter 4

VERSES

Poetry is not only dream and vision; it is the skeleton architecture of our lives.

Audre Lorde, Poetry is not a Luxury

A VERSE is a line of a poem. Poems can have two or three lines, sonnets must have fourteen lines, a haiku has three lines, and epic poems usually have thousands of lines. Some poems have rhymed verses and others have free verses. The structure of the poem depends on the poet's will. Poets decide how to convey the message. Some poetic lines can be fully understood, such as the first line of Shakespeare's Sonnet 18.

Example: Verse

Shall I compare thee to a summer's day?

WILLIAM SHAKESPEARE, Sonnet 18 (1609)

This poetic line has punctuation and the question is clear. The poet asks if he can compare someone to a sunny day. However, not every poetic line is an explicit idea. Most poets use enjambment. It is natural for most poets to write a line with just a fragment of a sentence, for instance, Emily Dickinson's first line

> Example: Verse
>
> To flee from a memory
>
>
> EMILY DICKINSON, To flee from memory' (1872)

It is just a fragment of a sentence. The verse brings some information but it is not enough to let us know much about the poem. We may ask, 'What is the poet talking about?' 'Is she referring to a specific moment?' 'What does it mean? Dickinson's verse is just part of an idea.

4.1   Enjambment

It is a literary device in which a thought or an idea is carried from one line to the other. It means that a verse may be a fragment of an idea, and the reader should keep reading the next verse to follow the train of thought. Enjambed verses often surprise readers. What comes next may confirm or contradict the previous thought.

> Example: Enjambment
>
> To flee from a memory
> Had we the Wings
> Many would fly
> Inured to slower things
> Birds with surprise
> Would scan the cowering Van

> Of men escaping
> From the mind of man
>
> **EMILY DICKINSON**, To flee from memory' (1872)

It is easier to understand what 'To flee from a memory' means as we read the subsequent verses. A person would like to have wings to fly away from memories. The image of memories escaping from the mind gives the idea of involuntary thoughts that haunt someone who feels fragile. The wings as a symbol of freedom let us know that the person feels imprisoned by memories, and not emotionally capable of facing the past. Considering that it takes a lot of courage to cope with some experiences, poetry becomes the wings she needs to fly.

4.2 Free Verse

Free verse does not follow any regulations concerning the length of the line, the number of syllables, or rhymes. It attracts poets who want to feel free from metrics and form to express an idea. Free verse follows the movement of thought and the poetic lines are arranged according to content rather than the rules of formal poetry. Rhythm, sound effects, and enjambment provide coherence to such poetry that follows the movement of thought or the pursuit of an idea with freedom.

It is worth noting that there is no predictable pattern in free verses, but there is certainly a natural rhythm of words.

> Free verse relies on images as a powerful vehicle to translate human experience and emotions.

Alliteration, anaphora, onomatopoeia, and other sound devices give a sense of balance and unity to the verses.

Since the first half of the twentieth century, free verse has flourished among great poets such as William Carlos Williams, Charles Bukowski, Sylvia Plath, Adrienne Rich, Ezra Pound, T. S. Eliot, Anne Sexton, and others. Writing in free verse might seem an aesthetic question, but it has political resonances. Breaking free from metrical rules can be a way of challenging societal conventions. This explains why poets who stand up against patriarchal authority, gender, and racial discrimination prefer free verses.

4.3   Let's read!

Belshazzar had a Letter –
He never had but one –
Belshazzar's Correspondent
Concluded and begun
In that immortal Copy
The Conscience of us all
Can read without its glasses
On Revelation's Wall

EMILY DICKINSON, Belshazzar had a letter (1890)

O God, O Venus, O Mercury, patron of thieves,
Give me in due time, I beseech you, a little tobacco-shop,
With the little bright boxes
piled up neatly upon the shelves
And the loose fragment cavendish
and the shag,
And the bright Virginia
loose under the bright glass cases,

And a pair of scales
  not too greasy,
    And the votailles dropping in for a word or two in passing,
     For a flip word, and to tidy their hair a bit.
      O God, O Venus, O Mercury, patron of thieves,
       Lend me a little tobacco-shop,
        or install me in any profession
         Save this damn'd profession of writing,
          where one needs one's brains all the time.

EZRA POUND, The Lake Isle (1916)

So you want to be a writer?
If it doesn't come bursting out of you
in spite of everything,
don't do it.
Unless it comes unasked out of your
heart and your mind and your mouth
and your gut,
don't do it.
If you have to sit for hours
Staring at your computer screen
Or hunched over your
Typewriter
Searching for words,
Don't do it.
If you're doing it for money or
Fame,
Don't do it
If you're doing it because you want
Women in your bed,
Don't do it.
If you have to sit there and

Rewrite it again and again,
Don't do it.
If it's hard working just thinking about doing it,
Don't do it.
If you're trying to write like somebody
Else,
Forget about it.
If you have to wait for it to roar out of
you,then wait patiently.
If it never does roar out of you,
do something else.
If you first have to read it to your wife
or your girlfriend or your boyfriend
or your parents or to anybody at all,
you're not ready.
Don't be like so many writers,
don't be like so many thousands of
people who call themselves writers,
don't be dull and boring and
pretentious, don't be consumed with self-
love.
the libraries of the world have
yawned themselves to
sleep
over your kind.
don't add to that.
don't do it.
unless it comes out of
your soul like a rocket,
unless being still would
drive you to madness or
suicide or murder,
don't do it.
unless the sun inside you is
burning your gut,

don't do it.
when it is truly time,
and if you have been chosen,
it will do it by
itself and it will keep on doing it
until you die or it dies in you.
there is no other way.
and there never was

CHARLES BUKOWSKI, So you want to be a writer? (1889)

4.4   Snapshot

Bukowsky's poem brings pieces of advice for those who want to be a poet. The poem is composed in free verses and looks like journalist writing. The content is clear and straightforward and it does not have rhymes or metrics. The number of syllables of each verse does not follow a pattern, however, the rhythm is present through sound effects.

Bukowski's rhythmic poem creates a musical pattern. It starts with a question to writers: 'So you want to be a writer?' The answers are marked by the repetition of 'Don't do it.' Although Bukowski does not ask any god to give him a tobacco shop to gain his life, as Ezra Pound does, he also advises that writing is not an easy task.

4.5 Practice

It's your turn

Get inspired by Bukowski and Ezra Pound and write some free verses. Don't forget that enjambment must play a very important role in your poem.

4.6 Poets

Charles Bukowski(1920- 1994)

was born in Germany and came to the United States at the age of two. He grew up in Los Angeles. Known as an anti-academic, Bukowski's poetry expresses the voices of the poor, the prostitutes the defeated, the demented, and the damned. In his free verses, he unravels his spontaneity and honesty. He died in March 1994.

Reference

Lorde, Audre. 'Poetry is not a Luxury' in Feminist Theory, edited by Wendy Kolmar and Frances Bartkowski. McGraw Hill: New York, 2005.

Chapter 5

RHYME

> Poetic knowledge is that which man spatters the
> object with all his mobilized riches.

> Aimé Cesáire, Poetry and Knowledge

CONSIDERED one of the main elements that differentiate
prose from poetry, it is commonplace to think rhymes
make poems sound more "poetical." Rhymes can be enchant-
ing, delighting, and sophisticated, but they can also be boring,
repetitive, and uncreative.

Rhymes cannot become an excuse for easy repetition pat-
terns that can ruin your poems.

It is worth noting that though rhyme calls the ear's atten-
tion, and sound makes verses easy to memorize, we need to
know how to control this tool. Rhymes can be perfect, im-
perfect, masculine, feminine, and internal. There is also eye
rhyme that cannot have much to do with sound but it attracts
the eyes.

5.1   Perfect Rhyme

Rhyme is perfect when the sounds of two words match exactly like mat/hat. We can find rhymes are everywhere; it is part of everyday language, children's games, nursery songs, marketing campaigns. Perfect rhymes can be classified as masculine and feminine.

Masculine Rhymes

Masculine rhymes have the stress in the last syllable like look/book. In the poem 'To any Reader,' Robert Louis Stevenson uses plenty of masculine rhymes – sees/trees, away/play, all/call, - to emphasize the importance of reading. It is a poem for children and rhymes make it light and fun.

Example: Masculine Rhyme

As from the house your mother sees
  You playing round the garden trees,
   So you may see, if you will look
    Through the windows of this book,
     Another child, far, far away,
      And in another garden, play.
       But do not think you can at all,
        By knocking on the window, call
         That child to hear you. He intent
          Is all on his play-business bent.
           He does not hear; he will not look,
            Nor yet be lured out of this book.
             For, long ago, the truth to say,
              He has grown up and gone away,
               And it is but a child of air
                That lingers in the garden there.

ROBERT LOUIS STEVENSON, To a Reader (1885)

Feminine Rhymes

Feminine Rhymes consist of two syllables, a stressed sylla-
ble followed by an unstressed one, as springest and wingest.

> Example: Feminine Rhyme
>
> Higher still and higher
> From the earth thou springest
>   Like a cloud of fire;
>   The blue deep thou wingest,
>   And singing still dost soar, and soaring ever singest.
>
> **Percy Shelley**, To a Skylark (1820)

5.2   Imperfect Rhyme

Imperfect rhymes, also called slant rhymes, do not match.
It is often a precarious rhyme as only a consonant sound or a
vowel sound may be connected. It is not easy to see words like
come and mists as rhyme, as in Dickinson's poem.

> Example: Imperfect Rhyme
>
> The Brooks laugh louder when I come
> The Breezes madder play
>   Wherefore mine eyes thy silver mists,
>   Wherefore, Oh Summer's Day?
>
> **EMILY DICKINSON**, The Bee is not afraid of me (1891)

5.3   Internal Rhyme

Internal rhyme is another technique a poet can use to give rhythm to the poem. This rhyme occurs within the line. In "The Raven," Edgar Alan Poe uses plenty of internal rhymes which bring suspense and rhythm to the poem.

> Example: Internal Rhyme
>
> Once upon a midnight dreary, while I pondered, weak and weary,
> Over many a quaint and curious volume of forgotten lore—
> While I nodded, nearly napping, suddenly there came a tapping,
> As of someone gently rapping, rapping at my chamber door.
>
> EDGAR ALLAN POE, The Raven (1845)

5.4   Eye Rhyme

An eye rhyme happens when two words have the same spelling but the pronunciation is different like bough and rough. The poet can simulate a rhyme in print but it sounds different as in Blake's example, eye and symmetry.

> Example: Eye Rhyme
>
> What immortal hand or eye,
>   Could frame thy fearful symmetry?
>
> WILLIAM BLAKE, The Tyger (1794)

5.5   Let's read!

My Faith is larger than the Hills—
 So when the Hills decay—
  My Faith must take the Purple Wheel
  To show the Sun the way—

'Tis first He steps upon the Vane—
 And then—upon the Hill—
  And then abroad the World He go
  To do His Golden Will—

And if His Yellow feet should miss—
 The Bird would not arise—
  The Flowers would slumber on their Stems—
  No Bells have Paradise—

How dare I, therefore, stint a faith
On which so vast depends—
Lest Firmament should fail for me—
The Rivet in the Bands

> **EMILY DICKINSON**, My Faith is larger than the Hills
>
> (1863)

Once upon a midnight dreary, while I pondered, weak and weary,
Over many a quaint and curious volume of forgotten lore—
While I nodded, nearly napping, suddenly there came a tapping,
As of some one gently rapping, rapping at my chamber door.
 "'Tis some visitor," I muttered, "tapping at my chamber door—
Only this and nothing more."

Ah, distinctly I remember it was in the bleak December;
  And each separate dying ember wrought its ghost upon the floor.
  Eagerly I wished the morrow;—vainly I had sought to borrow
    From my books surcease of sorrow—sorrow for the lost Lenore—
    For the rare and radiant maiden whom the angels name Lenore—
    Nameless here for evermore.

And the silken, sad, uncertain rustling of each purple curtain
  Thrilled me—filled me with fantastic terrors never felt before;
  So that now, to still the beating of my heart, I stood repeating
    "'Tis some visitor entreating entrance at my chamber door—
    Some late visitor entreating entrance at my chamber door;—
    This it is and nothing more."

Presently my soul grew stronger; hesitating then no longer,
  "Sir," said I, "or Madam, truly your forgiveness I implore;
  But the fact is I was napping, and so gently you came rapping,
    And so faintly you came tapping, tapping at my chamber door,
    That I scarce was sure I heard you"—here I opened wide the
door;—
    Darkness there and nothing more.

Deep into that darkness peering, long I stood there wondering, fear-
ing,
  Doubting, dreaming dreams no mortal ever dared to dream before;
  But the silence was unbroken, and the stillness gave no token,
    And the only word there spoken was the whispered word, "Lenore?"
    This I whispered, and an echo murmured back the word, "Lenore!"—
    Merely this and nothing more.

Back into the chamber turning, all my soul within me burning,
  Soon again I heard a tapping somewhat louder than before.
    "Surely," said I, "surely that is something at my window lattice;
    Let me see, then, what thereat is, and this mystery explore—
      Let my heart be still a moment and this mystery explore;—
        'Tis the wind and nothing more!"

Open here I flung the shutter, when, with many a flirt and flutter,
  In there stepped a stately Raven of the saintly days of yore;
    Not the least obeisance made he; not a minute stopped or stayed
he;
      But, with mien of lord or lady, perched above my chamber door—
      Perched upon a bust of Pallas just above my chamber door—
        Perched, and sat, and nothing more.

Then this ebony bird beguiling my sad fancy into smiling,
  By the grave and stern decorum of the countenance it wore,
    "Though thy crest be shorn and shaven, thou," I said, "art sure no
craven,
      Ghastly grim and ancient Raven wandering from the Nightly shore—
      Tell me what thy lordly name is on the Night's Plutonian shore!"
        Quoth the Raven "Nevermore."

Much I marvelled this ungainly fowl to hear discourse so plainly,
  Though its answer little meaning—little relevancy bore;
    For we cannot help agreeing that no living human being
      Ever yet was blessed with seeing bird above his chamber door—
      Bird or beast upon the sculptured bust above his chamber door,
        With such name as "Nevermore."

But the Raven, sitting lonely on the placid bust, spoke only
  That one word, as if his soul in that one word he did outpour.
    Nothing farther then he uttered—not a feather then he fluttered—
      Till I scarcely more than muttered "Other friends have flown be-
fore—
        On the morrow he will leave me, as my Hopes have flown before."
        Then the bird said "Nevermore."

Startled at the stillness broken by reply so aptly spoken,
  "Doubtless," said I, "what it utters is its only stock and store
    Caught from some unhappy master whom unmerciful Disaster
      Followed fast and followed faster till his songs one burden bore—
      Till the dirges of his Hope that melancholy burden bore
        Of 'Never—nevermore'."

But the Raven still beguiling all sad soul into smiling,
  Straight I wheeled a cushioned seat in front of bird, and bust and
door;
    Then, upon the velvet sinking, I betook myself to linking
      Fancy unto fancy, thinking what this ominous bird of yore—
      What this grim, ungainly, ghastly, gaunt, and ominous bird of yore
        Meant in croaking "Nevermore."

This I sat engaged in guessing, but no syllable expressing
  To the fowl whose fiery eyes now burned into my bosom's core;
    This and more I sat divining, with my head at ease reclining
      On the cushion's velvet-violet lining that the lamp-light gloated
o'er,
        But whose velvet-violet lining with the lamp-light gloating o'er,
        She shall press, ah, nevermore!

Then, methought, the air grew denser, perfumed from an unseen censer

Swung by Seraphim whose foot-falls tinkled on the tufted floor.

"Wretch," I cried, "thy God hath lent thee—by these angels he hath sent thee

Respite—respite and nepenthe from thy memories of Lenore;

Quaff, oh quaff this kind nepenthe and forget this lost Lenore!"

Quoth the Raven "Nevermore."

"Prophet!" said I, "thing of evil!—prophet still, if bird or devil!—

Whether Tempter sent, or whether tempest tossed thee here ashore,

Desolate yet all undaunted, on this desert land enchanted—

On this home by Horror haunted—tell me truly, I implore—

Is there—is there balm in Gilead?—tell me—tell me, I implore!"

Quoth the Raven "Nevermore."

"Prophet!" said I, "thing of evil!—prophet still, if bird or devil!

By that Heaven that bends above us—by that God we both adore—

Tell this soul with sorrow laden if, within the distant Aidenn,

It shall clasp a sainted maiden whom the angels name Lenore—

Clasp a rare and radiant maiden whom the angels name Lenore."

Quoth the Raven "Nevermore."

"Be that word our sign of parting, bird or friend!" I shrieked, upstarting—

"Get thee back into the tempest and the Night's Plutonian shore!

Leave no black plume as a token of that lie thy soul hath spoken!

Leave my loneliness unbroken!—quit the bust above my door!

Take thy beak from out my heart, and take thy form from off my door!"

Quoth the Raven "Nevermore."

And the Raven, never flitting, still is sitting, still is sitting
On the pallid bust of Pallas just above my chamber door;
And his eyes have all the seeming of a demon's that is dreaming,
And the lamp-light o'er him streaming throws his shadow on the
floor;
And my soul from out that shadow that lies floating on the floor
Shall be lifted—nevermore!

EDGAR ALLAN POE, The Raven (1845)

5.6   Practice

It's your turn

Find the internal rhymes in Poe's 'The Raven.' What
do they suggest?

5.7   Poets

Edgar Allan Poe (1809-1849)

was born in Boston and was a celebrated poet, and editor,
and author of horror stories. Poe was a kind of eccentric
man who tried alcohol and other drugs. Know as one
of the great American poets, Poe crafted his verses with
precision and perfection.

William Blake (1757 –1827)

was an English poet, painter, and printmaker. Largely un-
recognized during his life, Blake is now considered a semi-
nal figure in the history of the poetry and visual art of the

Romantic Age. What he called his prophetic works were said by 20th-century critic Northrop Frye to form "what is in proportion to its merits the least read body of poetry in the English language". Songs of Innocence (1789) and Songs of Experience (1794) are his major works which include the well-known poem "The Tyger.

Reference Cesáire, Aimé. 'Poetry and Knowledge' in Refusal of Shadow: Surrealism and the Caribbean, trans. by Michael Richardson and Krzysztof Fijalkowski, London:Verso, 1996

Chapter 6

RHYME SCHEME

> Rhyme, the rack of finest wits, That expresseth but by fits True conceit,
>
> ———————————————————————————
>
> Ben Johnson, A Fit of Rhyme Against Rhyme (1616)

A RHYME scheme is the pattern of rhymes at the end of the lines across a poem. It is often part of a tradition, for instance, a sonnet or a ballad follows specific patterns. However, it doesn't mean that a poet cannot create or experiment with any combination of rhymes. As you read the poem below, try to understand the rhyme scheme.

> **Example: Rhyme Scheme**
>
> Alone, I cannot be—
> For Hosts—do visit me—
>   Recordless Company—
>   Who baffle Key—
>
> **EMILY DICKINSON**, Alone I cannot be (1896)

We often identify a rhyme scheme using letters in alphabetical order. First, mark the first sound and label it as 'a', then, find similar sounds in the poem and label with the same letter. A different sound should be labeled 'b' and so forth. Read the poem again and see the rhyme pattern.

Example: a-a-a-a

Alone, I cannot be—[a]
  For Hosts—do visit me—[a]
    Recordless Company—[a]
    Who baffle Key—[a]

EMILY DICKINSON, Alone I cannot be (1896)

The rhyme scheme is usually notated with lowercase letters. When occurrences of the same sound appear in the subsequent verses of the poem, they should be labeled with the same letter. A line that does not rhyme receives an "x". Read the example and observe a different rhyme scheme.

Example: a-b-a-b

Although she feeds me bread of bitterness, [a]
And sinks into my throat her tiger's tooth, [b]
Stealing my breath of life, I will confess [a]
  I love this cultured hell that tests my youth. [b]

CLAUDE MCKAY, America (1921)

6.1   Monorhyme

It is the repetition of the same sound in every verse in a stanza or in the whole poem. It is usual to see the pattern in stanzas of three verses, as the one in Dickinson's poem,

Example: Monorhyme
A Spider sewed at Night [a]
Without a Light [a]
Upon an Arc of White [a]

EMILY DICKINSON, A Spider Sewed at Night (1891)

6.2   Envelope Rhyme

This rhyme scheme (abba) is relevant to stanza form in Petrachan sonnet. Here, line 1 rhymes with line 4 and line 2 rhymes with line 3.

Example: Envelope rhyme
If thou must love me, let it be for nought [a]
Except for love's sake only. Do not say [b]
I love her for her smile ... her look ... her way [b]
Of speaking gently, ... for a trick of thought [a]

ELIZABETH BARRET BROWNING, If thou must love me, ...
(1850)

6.3   Cross Rhyme

Cross rhyme is maybe the most popular pattern. It is used in Shakespearean sonnets. The rhyme scheme is abab.

> Example: Cross rhyme
>   Shall I compare thee to a summer's day? [a]
>   Thou art more lovely and more temperate: [b]
>   Rough winds do shake the darling buds of May, [a]
>   And summer's lease hath all too short a date; [b]
>
> **WILLIAM SHAKESPEARE**, Shall I Compare thee to summer's Day?

6.4   Let's read!

Alone, I cannot be—
  For Hosts—do visit me—
    Recordless Company—
    Who baffle Key—

They have no Robes, nor Names—
  No Almanacs—nor Climes—
    But general Homes
    Like Gnomes—

Their Coming, may be known
  By Couriers within—
    Their going—is not—
    For they've never gone—

                    EMILY DICKINSON, Alone I cannot be (1861)

In the old age, black was not counted fair,
 Or, if it were, it bore not beauty's name;
  But now is black beauty's successive heir,
   And beauty slandered with a bastard shame.
    For since each hand hath put on nature's power,
     Fairing the foul with art's false borrowed face,
      Sweet beauty hath no name, no holy bower,
       But is profaned, if not lives in disgrace.
        Therefore my mistress' eyes are raven black,
         Her eyes so suited, and they mourners seem
          At such who, not born fair, no beauty lack,
           Sland'ring creation with a false esteem.
            Yet so they mourn, becoming of their woe,
             That every tongue says beauty should look so.

WILLIAM SHAKESPEARE, Sonnet 127 (1609)

Take all my loves, my love, yea, take them all.
 What hast thou then more than thou hadst before?
  No love, my love, that thou mayst true love call;
   All mine was thine before thou hadst this more.
    Then, if for my love thou my love receivest,
     I cannot blame thee for my love thou usest;
      But yet be blamed if thou thyself deceivest
       By willful taste of what thyself refusest.
        I do forgive thy robb'ry, gentle thief,
         Although thou steal thee all my poverty;
          And yet love knows it is a greater grief
           To bear love's wrong than hate's known injury.
            Lascivious grace, in whom all ill well shows,
             Kill me with spites, yet we must not be foes.

WILLIAM SHAKESPEARE, Sonnet 40 (1609)

Although she feeds me bread of bitterness,
 And sinks into my throat her tiger's tooth,

Stealing my breath of life, I will confess
I love this cultured hell that tests my youth.
Her vigor flows like tides into my blood,
Giving me strength erect against her hate,
Her bigness sweeps my being like a flood.
Yet, as a rebel fronts a king in state,
I stand within her walls with not a shred
Of terror, malice, not a word of jeer.
Darkly I gaze into the days ahead,
And see her might and granite wonders there,
Beneath the touch of Time's unerring hand,
Like priceless treasures sinking in the sand.

CLAUDE MCKAY, America (1921)

Rhyme, the rack of finest wits,
That expresseth but by fits
True conceit,
Spoiling senses of their treasure,
Cozening judgment with a measure,
But false weight;
Wresting words from their true calling,
Propping verse for fear of falling
To the ground;
Jointing syllabes, drowning letters,
Fast'ning vowels as with fetters
They were bound!
Soon as lazy thou wert known,
All good poetry hence was flown,
And art banish'd.
For a thousand years together
All Parnassus' green did wither,
And wit vanish'd.
Pegasus did fly away,
At the wells no Muse did stay,

But bewail'd
So to see the fountain dry,
And Apollo's music die,
All light failed!
Starveling rhymes did fill the stage;
Not a poet in an age
Worth crowning;
Not a work deserving bays,
Not a line deserving praise,
Pallas frowning;
Greek was free from rhyme's infection,
Happy Greek by this protection
Was not spoiled.
Whilst the Latin, queen of tongues,
Is not yet free from rhyme's wrongs,
But rests foiled.
Scarce the hill again doth flourish,
Scarce the world a wit doth nourish
To restore
Phoebus to his crown again,
And the Muses to their brain,
As before.
Vulgar languages that want
Words and sweetness, and be scant
Of true measure,
Tyrant rhyme hath so abused,
That they long since have refused
Other cæsure.
He that first invented thee,
May his joints tormented be,
Cramp'd forever.
Still may syllabes jar with time,
Still may reason war with rhyme,
Resting never.
May his sense when it would meet

The cold tumor in his feet,
Grow unsounder;
And his title be long fool,
That in rearing such a school
Was the founder.

BEN JOHNSON, A Fit of Rhyme against Rhyme (1616)

Titan! to whose immortal eyes
 The sufferings of mortality,
  Seen in their sad reality,
   Were not as things that gods despise;
    What was thy pity's recompense?
     A silent suffering, and intense;
      The rock, the vulture, and the chain,
       All that the proud can feel of pain,
        The agony they do not show,
         The suffocating sense of woe,
          Which speaks but in its loneliness,
           And then is jealous lest the sky
            Should have a listener, nor will sigh
             Until its voice is echoless.

Titan! to thee the strife was given
 Between the suffering and the will,
  Which torture where they cannot kill;
   And the inexorable Heaven,
    And the deaf tyranny of Fate,
     The ruling principle of Hate,
      Which for its pleasure doth create
       The things it may annihilate,
        Refus'd thee even the boon to die:
         The wretched gift Eternity

Was thine—and thou hast borne it well.
All that the Thunderer wrung from thee
Was but the menace which flung back
On him the torments of thy rack;
The fate thou didst so well foresee,
But would not to appease him tell;
And in thy Silence was his Sentence,
And in his Soul a vain repentance,
And evil dread so ill dissembled,
That in his hand the lightnings trembled.

Thy Godlike crime was to be kind,
To render with thy precepts less
The sum of human wretchedness,
And strengthen Man with his own mind;
But baffled as thou wert from high,
Still in thy patient energy,
In the endurance, and repulse
Of thine impenetrable Spirit,
Which Earth and Heaven could not convulse,
A mighty lesson we inherit:
Thou art a symbol and a sign
To Mortals of their fate and force;
Like thee, Man is in part divine,
A troubled stream from a pure source;
And Man in portions can foresee
His own funereal destiny;
His wretchedness, and his resistance,
And his sad unallied existence:
To which his Spirit may oppose
Itself—and equal to all woes,
And a firm will, and a deep sense,
Which even in torture can descry
Its own concenter'd recompense,

Triumphant where it dares defy,
And making Death a Victory.

LORD BYRON, Prometheus (1816)

6.5   Practice

It's your turn

Rewrite your poems. Try some rhymed verses.

6.6   Poets

Ben Jonson (1572- 1637)
was an English Renaissance playwright, poet, actor and literary player. He is best known for his satirical plays and lyric poetry.

Robert Louis Stevenson (1850- 1894)
was born in the United Kingdom and was a novelist, poet and essayist and travel writer. His most famous works are Treasure Island, The Strange Case of Dr. Jekyll and Mr. Hyde and A Child's Garden of Verses.

Elizabeth Barrett Browning (1806 - 1861)
was an English poet of the Victorian era, popular in Britain and the United States during her lifetime. She wrote poetry from the age of eleven. Her first adult collection of poems was published in 1838 and she wrote prolifically between 1841 and 1844, producing poetry, translation and prose. Elizabeth's volume Poems (1844) brought her great success, attracting the admiration of the writer Robert Browning. Their correspondence, courtship and marriage

were carried out in secret, for fear of her father's disapproval. Following the wedding she was indeed disinherited by her father. In 1846, the couple moved to Italy, where she would live for the rest of her life.

Derek Alton Walcott (1930 – 2017)

was a poet and playwright from Saint Lucia. He received the 1992 the Nobel prize in Literature. He was the University of Alberta's first distinguished scholar in residence, where he taught undergraduate and graduate writing courses. He also served as Professor of Poetry at the University of Essex from 2010 to 2013. His works include the Homeric epic poem Omeros (1990), which many critics view "as Walcott's major achievement. In addition to winning the Nobel Prize, Walcott received many literary awards over the course of his career.

Claude McKay (1890 –1948)

became a central figure in the Harlem Renaissance. Born in Jamaica, McKay first traveled to the United States to attend college, and encountered W. E. B. Du Bois's The Souls of Black Folk which stimulated McKay's interest in political involvement. He moved to New York City in 1914 and in 1919 wrote "If We Must Die", one of his best known works, a widely reprinted sonnet responding to the wave of white-on-black race riots and lynchings following the conclusion of the First World War.

Chapter 7

SONNET

Self-being is only real in communication with
another self-being.

Karl Jaspers, Philosophy of Existence

THROUGH ages and across cultures, sonnets have become
the most popular form among poets. A sonnet contains a
sophisticated rhyme scheme in which the poet combines beau-
tiful sound with meaningful content.

Thomas Wyatt introduced the sonnet to English Litera-
ture in the sixteenth century by translating or imitating
Petrarch's sonnets.

Wyatt evolved to create his sonnets, slightly different from
the form used by Italian writers. A sonnet contains fourteen
lines and two parts. The first part regards the argument or
a question and the second one is the conclusion, called the
volta, meaning turn. The volta summarizes the whole idea
and concludes the poem, suggesting a shift in the idea that
can be an answer, a progression, or an antithesis.

It is worth noting that, despite having two parts, a sonnet always appears in print as an arrangement of fourteen lines altogether. In English poetry, sonnets can be Petrarchan (named after Petrarch) and Shakesperean (named after Shakespeare).

7.1 Petrarchan Sonnet

The Petrarchan sonnet has fourteen lines, which contain an octave and one sestet. An octave is a group of eight lines, containing the rhyme scheme abba abba. (enclosed or envelope rhymes) A sestet is a group of six lines, containing the rhyme scheme cdc dcd (terza rima) or cde cde. In this format, the sestet, the last six lines, concludes the sonnet with a shift or a turn in the argument, known as volta.

Example: Petrarchan sonnet
If thou must love me, let it be for nought [a]
Except for love's sake only. Do not say [b]
I love her for her smile ... her look ... her way [b]
Of speaking gently, ... for a trick of thought [a]
That falls in well with mine, and certes brought [a]
A sense of pleasant ease on such a day'— [b]
For these things in themselves, Belovèd, may [b]
Be changed, or change for thee,and love, so wrought, [a]
May be unwrought so. Neither love me for [c]
Thine own dear pity's wiping my cheeks dry,— [d]
A creature might forget to weep, who bore [c]
Thy comfort long, and lose thy love thereby! [d]
But love me for love's sake, that evermore [c]
Thou may'st love on, through love's eternity. [d]

ELIZABETH BARRET BROWNING, If thou must love me (1850)

7.2   Shakespearean Sonnet or English Sonnet

William Shakespeare's sonnets, printed in 1609, caused a lot of speculation regarding his controversial themes, such as homosexuality, politics, and so forth. Unlike the Petrarchan, Shakespeare's sonnet does not contain one octave and one sestet. It has three quatrains, a quatrain is a block of verses containing four lines, and a couplet, a block of two lines. In Shakesperean sonnets, the poet concludes his idea with the volta in the last two lines. This shift does not come without a surprise or an unexpected answer.

Example: Shakespearean sonnet
Shall I compare thee to a Summer's day? [a]
Thou art more lovely and more temperate: [b]
Rough winds do shake the darling buds of May, [a]
And summer's lease hath all too short a date: [b]
Sometime too hot the eye of heaven shines, [c]
And often is his gold complexion dimm'd,[d]
And every fair from fair sometimes declines,[c]
By chance or nature's changing course untrimm'd: [d]
But thy eternal summer shall not fade [e]
Nor lose possession of that fair thou ow'st, [f]
Nor shall Death brag thou wander'st in his shade,[e]
When in eternal lines to time thou grow'st: [f]
So Long as men can breathe or eyes can see, [g]
So long lives this, and this gives life to thee. [g]

WILLIAM SHAKESPEARE, Shall I compare you to summer's day?
(1609)

7.3   Let's read!

If we must die, let it not be like hogs
  Hunted and penned in an inglorious spot,
    While round us bark the mad and hungry dogs,
    Making their mock at our accursèd lot.
    If we must die, O let us nobly die,
      So that our precious blood may not be shed
      In vain; then even the monsters we defy
        Shall be constrained to honor us though dead!
        O kinsmen! we must meet the common foe!
        Though far outnumbered let us show us brave,
        And for their thousand blows deal one death-blow!
        What though before us lies the open grave?
          Like men we'll face the murderous, cowardly pack,
          Pressed to the wall, dying, but fighting back!

CLAUDE MCKAY, If we must die (1919)

Whoso list to hunt, I know where is an hind,
  But as for me, hélas, I may no more.
    The vain travail hath wearied me so sore,
    I am of them that farthest cometh behind.
    Yet may I by no means my wearied mind
      Draw from the deer, but as she fleeth afore
      Fainting I follow. I leave off therefore,
        Sithens in a net I seek to hold the wind.
        Who list her hunt, I put him out of doubt,
        As well as I may spend his time in vain.
        And graven with diamonds in letters plain
          There is written, her fair neck round about:

Noli me tangere, for Caesar's I am,
And wild for to hold, though I seem tame.

THOMAS WYATT, Whoso list to hunt (1550)

My mistress' eyes are nothing like the sun;
 Coral is far more red than her lips' red;
 If snow be white, why then her breasts are dun;
 If hairs be wires, black wires grow on her head:
 I have seen roses damask'd, red and white.
 But no such roses see I in her cheeks;
 And in some perfumes is there more delight
 Than in the breath that from my mistress reeks:
 I love to hear her speak, yet well I know
 That music hath a far more pleasing sound;
 I grant I never saw a goddess go,
 My mistress when she walks treads on the ground.
 And yet by heaven I think my love as rare
 As any she belied with false compare.

WILLIAM SHAKESPEARE, Sonnet 130 (1609)

7.4   Snapshot

Elizabeth Barret Browning's sonnet 'If thou must love me, let it be for nought,' is a Petrarchan sonnet. It has two parts: an octave and a sestet. Though the poem brings love as its main theme, it also breaks with the idea of the sonnet as a way of expressing love. In many ways, the poem deconstructs the idea of an ideal woman, stating men usually love women who encapsulate in their personalities some patriarchal concepts that structure their lives. For instance, patriarchal societies expect from women a certain 'look,' 'smile' and way 'of speaking gently.'

In the first part of the poem called an octave, the poet exposes that a woman should not carry artificial femininity in search of love because real love cannot rely on ideal femininity. She refuses this love, pointing out, through a feminist lesson, what a woman does not expect from a male partner. The poet voices the desire of love for love's sake, a sentiment that must be deep, strong, and invisible. This love resists conceptualization, explanation, or gender expectation. It is pure and genuine, and a matching of souls that resists anything and goes on through eternity.

In the first part of 'Sonnet 18,' the poet presents a problem, an unsolved situation in three quatrains (three stanzas of four lines). First, the poet states a problem, "Can the beloved person be compared to a summer's day?" Each quatrain adds a new idea to the main problem. 'Thou art more lovely and more temperate:" or "Rough winds do shake the darling buds of May/ And summer's lease hath all too short a date.' The poet explains that sometimes the weather is too hot and not very pleasant, unlike the beloved person who is always cool and never bothers him.

The next quatrain brings another image to add to this comparison. The sun declines and disappears. And every fair from fair sometimes declines/By chance or nature's changing course untrimm'd:" Summer is ephemeral and life is ephemeral too as the shadow of death extinguishes its light. The answer for death comes in the last couplet as the poet states that 'So Long as men can breathe or eyes can see/So long lives this, and this gives life to thee." As the sonnet remains forever, the beloved person gains eternal life through the verses of this poem that is going to remain alive in the hearts and minds of those who love poetry.

7.5 Practice

It's your turn

Identify the volta in each sonnet and explain it.

7.6 Poets

William Shakespeare

a poet, playwright and actor of the Renaissance. His most celebrated works include the plays Hamlet, Macbeth and King Lear, and his sonnets. He is regarded as the greatest writer in the English language and the world's most influential dramatist. Shakespeare was born and raised in Stratford-upon-Avon, Warwickshire. At the age of 18, he married Anne Hathaway, with whom he had three children. Sometime between 1585 and 1592, he began a successful career in London as an actor, writer, and part-owner of a playing company called the Lord Chamberlain's Men, later known as the King's Men. At age 49 (around 1613), he appears to have retired to Stratford, where he died three years later. Few records of Shakespeare's private life survive; this has stimulated considerable speculation about such matters as his physical appearance, his sexuality, his religious beliefs and whether the works attributed to him were written by others.

Sir Thomas Wyatt (1503 –1542)

was a 16th-century English politician, ambassador, and lyric poet credited with introducing the sonnet to English literature. He was born at Allington Castle near Maidstone in Kent, though the family was originally from

Yorkshire. His family adopted the Lancastrian side in the Wars of Roses. His father who had earlier been imprisoned and tortured by Richard III, had been a Privy Councillor of Henry VII and remained a trusted adviser when Henry VIII ascended the throne in 1509. In public life his principal patron was Thomas Cromwell, after whose death he was recalled from abroad and imprisoned (1541).

Reference

Jaspers, Karl. Philosophy of Existence. Existenzphilosophie, Berlin: de Gruyter. Translated as Philosophy of Existence, trans. R. F. Grabau, Philadelphia: University of Pennsylvania Press, 1971.

Chapter 8

STRESS

The light of a lamp does not flicker in a windless
place

Bhagavad-Gita, Song of God

T O WRITE a sonnet, poets should follow a strict rhyme
scheme, choose between Petrarchan and Shakesperean for-
mations, and count fourteen lines. It is not all. There is
still one important detail about sonnets. They are written in
iambic pentameter. An iamb means a group of two syllables
one unstressed and one stressed, forming one foot or one beat.
The word pentameter means that each line of a sonnet must
have five iambs.

In English poetry, the meter of a line can be syllabic, allit-
erative, or accentual- syllabic. In syllabic verses, the number of
syllables determines the length of the line. Alliterative verses
have four stresses, irrespective of the number of syllables, two
stresses before and two after a pause (a caesura) at the center
of the line. Same consonant sounds at the beginning of words
mark the stressed syllables. Accentual- syllabic verses, the
most usual in English poetry, combine the number of syllables

with the number of stresses.

8.1   Iambic Pentameter

Iamb is the natural rhythm you talk in English language. That is why so many poets choose to write in iambs, including Shakespeare. An iamb is a unit that forms the poetic line. Each one of these units forms one foot. Pentameter refers to number five. Thus, a verse of a sonnet has five syllabic groups, each one containing the pattern of one unstressed syllable followed by a stressed syllable. An example of an iamb is the word away. It has two syllables: a/way and the second stressed. This verse from sonnet 18 has five feet.

Example: Iambic Pentameter
To be, or not to be, that is the question

WILLIAM SHAKESPEARE, Hamlet (1609)

Not all verses follow this meter, but it has been one of the favorite metric formations because it follows the natural rhythm of English language. Pentameter refers to five feet, the length of the line can vary. For instance, ballads are often written in trimeter or tetratmeter.

Monometer – one foot.
Dimeter – two feet
Trimeter – three feet
Tetrameter – four feet
Pentameter – five feet
Hexameter – six feet
Heptameter – seven feet

Iambic Tetrameter It has four feet as in the example.

Example: Iambic Tetrameter
My mother thinks us long away;

My *mo*/ther *thinks*/us *long*/a *way*

A. E. HOUSMAN, Farewell to Barn and Stack and Tree (1896)

Iambic Trimeter

Observe the line "To-night she'll be alone." It has six sylla-
bles, divided into three syllabic groups of one unaccented and
one accented. It is an iambic trimester.

Example:
(To-*night*/ she'll *be*/ a-*lone*)

Other syllabic feet in English poetry

Besides iamb, there are meters in English that you should
know. Iamb is just one that is very used by poets. It is good
to know other four kinds of accentual- syllabic verses.

Anapest

Two unaccented syllables followed by an accented syllable
as in the word in/ter/**vene** as in the verses of Edgar Allan
Poe's Ulalume.

Example: Anapest
It was night in the lonesome October
Of my most immemorial year

It was *night*/ in the *lone*/some Oc*to*/ber

Of my *most*/ imme*mo*/rial year

EDGAR ALLAN POE, Ulalume (1847)

Trochee

A trochee has a stressed syllable followed by an unstressed one. It reverses the iamb. As in the word **on**/ly. Longfellow's poem is trochaic tetrameter, defective in the fourth verse.

Example: Trochee

Tell me not, in mournful numbers

Life is but an empty dream

For the soul is dead that slumbers

And things are not what they seem

Tell me/ *not*, in /*mournful*/ *num*/bers

Life is/ *but* an/ *empty*/ *dream*

For the /*soul* is /*dead* that/ *slum*bers

And things/ *are* not /*what* they /*seem*

H.W.Longfellow, Psalm of Life (1838)

Dactyl

It is a three-syllable foot, one stressed followed by two unstressed syllables, as in the word happily *hap*/pi/ly. Observe the dactylic hexameter in Longfellow's Evangeline:

Example: Dactyl

This is the forest primeval, the murmuring pines and the hemlocks

This is the /*forest* pri/*me*val, the/ *mur*muring/

*pi*nes and the /*hem*locks

H.W. LONGFELLOW, Evangeline(1847)

8.2   Controversial English Feet

Spondee and Pyrrhic

A spondee is a two-syllable foot, both stressed like the words **day task** and **football**, but if stressed and unstressed syllables form one foot, how could this work? Only compound words have two stresses. Some argue spondee cannot exist in the English language.

Pyrrhic is a two-syllable foot, both unstressed. This case is a bit worse than spondee because it is not possible to think of a word with two unstressed syllables as tresses always fall on one syllable.

8.3   Let's read!

This is the forest primeval. The murmuring pines and the hemlocks,
  Bearded with moss, and in garments green, indistinct in the twilight,
    Stand like Druids of eld, with voices sad and prophetic,
      Stand like harpers hoar, with beards that rest on their bosoms.
        Loud from its rocky caverns, the deep-voiced neighboring ocean
          Speaks, and in accents disconsolate answers the wail of the forest.

This is the forest primeval; but where are the hearts that beneath it
  Leaped like the roe, when he hears in the woodland the voice of the huntsman?
    Where is the thatch-roofed village, the home of Acadian farmers,–

Men whose lives glided on like rivers that water the woodlands,
　Darkened by shadows of earth, but reflecting an image of heaven?
　Waste are those pleasant farms, and the farmers forever departed!
　　Scattered like dust and leaves, when the mighty blasts of Octo-
ber
　　　Seize them, and whirl them aloft, and sprinkle them far o'er
the ocean
　　　　Naught but tradition remains of the beautiful village of Grand-
Pré.

Ye who believe in affection that hopes, and endures, and is patient,
　Ye who believe in the beauty and strength of woman's devotion,
　List to the mournful tradition, still sung by the pines of the forest;
　List to a Tale of Love in Acadie, home of the happy.

　　　　　　　　H.W. LONGFELLOW, Evangeline' (1847)

Tell me not, in mournful numbers,
　Life is but an empty dream!
　For the soul is dead that slumbers,
　　And things are not what they seem.

Life is real! Life is earnest!
　And the grave is not its goal;
　Dust thou art, to dust returnest,
　　Was not spoken of the soul.

Not enjoyment, and not sorrow,
　Is our destined end or way;
　But to act, that each to-morrow

Find us farther than to-day.

Art is long, and Time is fleeting,
  And our hearts, though stout and brave,
    Still, like muffled drums, are beating
      Funeral marches to the grave.

In the world's broad field of battle,
  In the bivouac of Life,
    Be not like dumb, driven cattle!
    Be a hero in the strife!

Trust no Future, howe'er pleasant!
  Let the dead Past bury its dead!
    Act,— act in the living Present!
      Heart within, and God o'erhead!

Lives of great men all remind us
  We can make our lives sublime,
    And, departing, leave behind us
      Footprints on the sands of time;

Footprints, that perhaps another,
  Sailing o'er life's solemn main,
    A forlorn and shipwrecked brother,
      Seeing, shall take heart again.

Let us, then, be up and doing,
  With a heart for any fate;
    Still achieving, still pursuing,
      Learn to labor and to wait.

H.W. LONGFELLOW, Psalm of Life (1838)

In the morning I walked in Santillana
 Under a sky crystal and cobalt
  Shot with the arrow heads of swifts,
   Santillana half-dead city of flies,
    Reeking of cow dung splashed on broken cobbles,
    Half-dead city — O florid heraldries
     Stonily boasting the pride of dead hidalgos.

Santillana!
 Your lordly balconies are red
  With the common flowers of your servants' sons.
    . . .
    None to walk the streets and the cloister
     With sword or prayer for the glory of God and Spain
     . . .
      O noble lords, your tombs are broken,
       Horrors of filth and common rubbish
        Mix with princely dust.

RICHARD ALDINGTON, Santillana (1935)

8.4   Snapshot

The iambic foot is the most popular in English because it follows the natural rhythm of the English language, providing a conversational tone to poetry. Besides iamb, there are other feet in English poetry, as we discussed in this chapter. They can be anapest, trochee, dactyl, and so forth. Not all verses need to have five feet, as the lines of a sonnet, but metrical lines can be dimeter, trimeter, tetrameter. Writing poetry is like composing a song, the musician chooses the rhythm, tone, images, and combines elements that altogether contribute to harmony. Poetry brings together elements that stimulate not only sight and hearing, but also smell, taste, and touch, arranged in a way the reader can perceive the world the poet is picturing through the verses of a sonnet or a ballad.

8.5   Practice

It's your turn

Choose one of your poems and rewrite a couple of lines, combining meter and rhyme.

8.6   Poets

Henry Wadsworth Longfellow (1807-1882)
was an American poet and educator whose works include "Paul Revere's Ride", "The Song of Hiwatha," and "Evangeline." He was the first American to translate Dante Alighieri's Divina Comedia in Portland, Maine, then a district of Massachusetts.

Richard Aldington (1892 –1962)
was an English writer and poet, and an early associate of the Imagist movement. He was married to the poet Hilda Doolittle (H. D.) from 1911 to 1938. His 50-year writing career covered poetry, novels, criticism and biography. He edited The Egoist, a literary journal, and wrote for The Times Literary Supplement, Vogue, The Criterion and Poetry. His contacts included writers like T. S. Eliot, D. H. Lawrence, Ezra Pound, W. B. Yeats, Lawrence Durrell and C. P. Snow. He championed Hilda Doolittle as the major poetic voice of the Imagist movement and helped her work gain international notice.

Reference

Bhagavad-Gita, Song of God translated by Swami Prabhavananda and Christopher Isherwood.

Chapter 9

STANZAS

> If you will have the requisite energy, you can win
> what is the chief in life, win yourself, acquire
> yourself.

Soren Kierkegaard, Either/Or

A BLOCK of verses defined by its arrangement of meter and rhymes, stanzas follow a pattern and a train of thought. With the same number of lines across the poem, stanzas create a sense of organization of thought, analogous to the paragraph in prose. However, much more than a form of organizing the poet's thought, stanzas contribute to the rhythm and sound effects.

Some poets do not follow strict patterns regarding rhyme schemes, as in the first stanzas of Gwendolyn Brooks' "Rudolph Reed" and Emily Dickinson's "The Brain is wider than the sky." These stanzas do not have rigid schemes but they contain imperfect rhymes, alliteration, anaphora, and images as a means of putting the ideas together. In the first quatrain of her poem, Brooks rhymes oaken/man and too/grew, using an imperfect rhyme to form a pattern. Dickinson also experiments with rhyme patterns, using imperfect rhymes or letting some lines unrhymed.

Example:
 Rudolph Reed was oaken.
His wife was oaken too.
And his two good girls and his good little man
Oakened as they grew.

GWENDOLYN BROOKS, The Ballad of Rudolph Reed (1963)

Example:
 The Brain – is wider than the Sky –
For – put them side by side –
The one the other will contain
With ease – and You- beside –

The Brain is deeper than the sea –
For- hold them Blue and Blue –
The one the other will absorb –
As Sponges – Buckets – do

The Brain is just the weight of God—
For—Heft them—Pound for Pound—
And they will differ—if they do—
As Syllable from Sound—

EMILY DICKINSON, ,

The Brain is wider than the Sky (1862)

A stanza can have two lines, three, four, or twelve lines, it depends on the poet anf how the ideas fit in the block of verses. The most popular stanzas in English poetry are couplets and quatrains. Longer stanzaic forms with eight or more lines usually combine shorter stanzas as quatrains and couplets.

9.1   Couplet

It is a two-line stanza. Known as the most popular stanzaic form in English poetry, couplets can be open, closed, and heroic.

Closed couplets

They express a complete thought and bring punctuation at the end of the second line.

> Example: Closed couplets
> O write it not, my hand—the name appears
> Already written—wash it out, my tears!
>
> **ALEXANDER POPE**, Eloisa to Abelard (1717)

Open couplets

At the end of the second line, open couplets have an enjambment. The idea flows into the next couplets.

Example: Open couplets
A sense of pleasant ease on such a day –
For these things in themselves, Beloved, may

ELIZABETH BARRET BROWNING, If thou must love me, ...
(1850)

Heroic couplets

They are closed couplets, written in iambic pentameter. They have rigid rhymes and fixed length of the line.

Example: Heroic couplets
Whan that Aprille with his shoures soote,
The droghte of March hath perced to the roote,

And bathed every veyne in swich licóur
Of which vertú engendred is the flour;

Whan Zephirus eek with his swete breeth
Inspired hath in every holt and heeth

GEOFFREY CHAUCER, The Canterbury Tales (1392-95)

9.2   Tercet

A tercet is a three-line stanza that can be a triplet or a terza rima, depending on the rhyme scheme.

Triplet

It is a three-line stanza with rhyme scheme a-a-a b-b-b c-c-c, as in Emily Dickinson's poem. This triplet has a slight variation in the second and third stanzas which breaks the strict rule with imperfect rhymes.

Example: Triplet
A Spider sewed at Night
Without a Light
Upon an Arc of White.

If Ruff it was of Dame
Or Shroud of Gnome
Himself himself inform.

Of Immortality
His Strategy
Was Physiognomy.

EMILY DICKINSON, A Spider Sewed at Night (1891)

TERZA RIMA It is a three line stanza with a fixed number of lines, often a tetrameter or a pentameter. The rhyme scheme is aBa bCb cDc dEd, and so on. In each stanza, the rhyme in the second line forms the outside rhymes of the next stanza. For example, observe how in the third stanza of Shelley's poem, until rhymes with fill and hill in the fourth stanza.

Example: Terza Rima
The winged seeds, where they lie cold and low,
Each like a corpse within its grave, until Thine
azure sister of the Spring shall blow

Her clarion o'er the dreaming earth, and fill Driv-

ing sweet buds like flocks to feed in air With
living hues and odours plain and hill:

PERCY SHELLEY, Ode to the West Wing (1820)

9.3 Quatrain

It is a four-line stanza. One of most typical stanzas in English poetry, quatrains have different rhyme schemes. They can be formed as a-a-a-a- (monorhyme), a-a-b-b (paired couplets), abba (envelope rhyme), and a-b-a-b (cross rhyme)

Paired Couplets The rhyme scheme in the quatrains of William Bake's poem is aabb.

Example: Paired couplets

Tyger Tyger, burning bright
In the forests of the night,
  What immortal hand or eye
    Could frame thy fearful symmetry?

In what distant deeps or skies
  Burnt the fire of thine eyes?
    On what wings dare he aspire?
    What the hand dare seize the fire?

And what shoulder and what art
  Could twist the sinews of thy heart?
    And when thy heart began to beat,
      What dread hand and what dread feet?

What the hammer? What the chain?
  In what furnace was thy brain?
    What the anvil? What dread grasp

Dare its deadly terrors clasp?

When the stars threw down their spears,
 And water'd heaven with their tears,
  Did He smile His work to see?
  Did He who made the lamb make thee?

Tyger Tyger burning bright
 In the forests of the night,
  What immortal hand or eye
  Dare frame thy fearful symmetry?

WILLIAM BLAKE, The Tyger (1794)

-

The rhyme scheme a-b-a-b is the most common quatrain rhyme.

Example:
 I wander thro' each charter'd street,
  Near where the charter'd Thames does flow.
   And mark in every face I meet
    Marks of weakness, marks of woe.

In every cry of every Man,
 In every Infants cry of fear,
  In every voice: in every ban,
   The mind-forg'd manacles I hear

How the Chimney-sweepers cry
 Every blackning Church appalls,
  And the hapless Soldiers sigh
   Runs in blood down Palace walls

But most thro' midnight streets I hear
  How the youthful Harlots curse
    Blasts the new-born Infants tear
    And blights with plagues the Marriage hearse

WILLIAM BLAKE, London (1794

9.4   Cinquain

It is a five-line stanza. The rhyme may have many variations as it combines shorter stanzas, such as couplets, and tercets.

Example:

I love to rise in a summer morn,
  When the birds sing on every tree;
    The distant huntsman winds his horn,
    And the skylark sings with me:
      O what sweet company!

But to go to school in a summer morn, -
  O it drives all joy away!
    Under a cruel eye outworn,
      The little ones spend the day
      In sighing and dismay.

Ah then at times I drooping sit,
  And spend many an anxious hour;
    Nor in my book can I take delight,
      Nor sit in learning's bower,
        Worn through with the dreary shower.

How can the bird that is born for joy
  Sit in a cage and sing?
   How can a child, when fears annoy,
    But droop his tender wing,
     And forget his youthful spring!

O father and mother if buds are nipped,
 And blossoms blown away;
  And if the tender plants are stripped
   Of their joy in the springing day,
    By sorrow and care's dismay, -

How shall the summer arise in joy,
 Or the summer fruits appear?
  Or how shall we gather what griefs destroy,
   Or bless the mellowing year,
    When the blasts of winter appear?

WILLIAM BLAKE, The School Boy (1794)

9.5   Sestain

It is a six-line stanza. It is often a combination of shorter stanzas. Sesta Rima is an arrangement with the rhyme scheme ababcc, a quatrain and a couplet.

Example:
 I wandered lonely as a cloud
  That floats on high o'er vales and hills,
   When all at once I saw a crowd,
    A host, of golden daffodils;

Beside the lake, beneath the trees,
Fluttering and dancing in the breeze.

Continuous as the stars that shine
And twinkle on the milky way,
They stretched in never-ending line
Along the margin of a bay:
Ten thousand saw I at a glance,
Tossing their heads in sprightly dance.

The waves beside them danced; but they
Out-did the sparkling waves in glee:
A poet could not but be gay,
In such a jocund company:
I gazed—and gazed—but little thought
What wealth the show to me had brought:

For oft, when on my couch I lie
In vacant or in pensive mood,
They flash upon that inward eye
Which is the bliss of solitude;
And then my heart with pleasure fills,
And dances with the daffodils.

WILLIAM WORDSWORTH, I Wandered Lonely as a Cloud (1815)

A variation of sesta rima is the 'Venus and Adonis' stanza, written in iambic pentameter. In the example, Dickinson reverses the order. Her poem is a couplet followed by a quatrain.

Example:

Bring me the sunset in a cup,
 Reckon the morning's flagons up
  And say how many Dew,
   Tell me how far the morning leaps –
    Tell me what time the weaver sleeps
     Who spun the breadths of blue!

Write me how many notes there be
 In the new Robin's ecstasy
  Among astonished boughs –
   How many trips the Tortoise makes –
    How many cups the Bee partakes,
     The Debauchee of Dews!

Also, who laid the Rainbow's piers,
 Also, who leads the docile spheres
  By withes of supple blue?
   Whose fingers string the stalactite –
    Who counts the wampum of the night
     To see that none is due?

Who built this Little Alban House
 And shut the windows down so close
  My spirit cannot see?
   Who'll let me out some gala day
    With implements to fly away,
     Passing Pomposity?

EMILY DICKINSON, Bring me the sunset in a cup (1891)

9.6   Longer Stanzas

Septet

It is a seven-line stanza. A rigid septet is the Rime Royal, a seven-line stanza with a fixed-line length (iambic pentameter) and the rhyme scheme a-b-a-b-b-c-c.

Example:

FROM off a hill whose concave womb reworded
A plaintful story from a sistering vale,
  My spirits to attend this double voice accorded,
  And down I laid to list the sad-tuned tale;
  Ere long espied a fickle maid full pale,
    Tearing of papers, breaking rings a-twain,
    Storming her world with sorrow's wind and rain.

    ...

'For, lo, his passion, but an art of craft,
  Even there resolved my reason into tears;
  There my white stole of chastity I daff'd,
  Shook off my sober guards and civil fears;
    Appear to him, as he to me appears,
      All melting; though our drops this difference bore,
      His poison'd me, and mine did him restore.

'In him a plenitude of subtle matter,
  Applied to cautels, all strange forms receives,
  Of burning blushes, or of weeping water,
    Or swooning paleness; and he takes and leaves,
    In either's aptness, as it best deceives,
      To blush at speeches rank to weep at woes,
      Or to turn white and swoon at tragic shows.

'That not a heart which in his level came
Could 'scape the hail of his all-hurting aim,
Showing fair nature is both kind and tame;
And, veil'd in them, did win whom he would maim:
Against the thing he sought he would exclaim;
When he most burn'd in heart-wish'd luxury,
He preach'd pure maid, and praised cold chastity.

...

WILLIAM SHAKESPEARE, A Lover's Complaint (1609)

Eight- line stanza

An octet is an eight-line stanza. It is often mixing of quatrains and couplets. The Ottava Rima, a rigid form written in iambic pentameter, follows the rhyme scheme abababcc in which the first six lines are cross-rhymed, followed by a couplet, as in Lord Byron's Don Juan.

Example:

Bob Southey! You're a poet, poet laureate,
And representative of all the race.
Although 'tis true that you turned out a Tory at
Last, yours has lately been a common case.
And now my epic renegade, what are ye at
With all the lakers, in and out of place?
A nest of tuneful persons, to my eye
Like four and twenty blackbirds in a pye,

Which pye being opened they began to sing'
(This old song and new simile holds good),
A dainty dish to set before the King'
Or Regent, who admires such kind of food.
And Coleridge too has lately taken wing,

But like a hawk encumbered with his hood,
    Explaining metaphysics to the nation.
    I wish he would explain his explanation.

You, Bob, are rather insolent, you know,
  At being disappointed in your wish
    To supersede all warblers here below,
      And be the only blackbird in the dish.
      And then you overstrain yourself, or so,
        And tumble downward like the flying fish
          Gasping on deck, because you soar too high,
            Bob, And fall for lack of moisture quite a dry Bob.

                                    LORD BYRON, Don Juan (1837)

Ten-line stanza

Example:

Thou still unravish'd bride of quietness,
  Thou foster-child of silence and slow time,
    Sylvan historian, who canst thus express
      A flowery tale more sweetly than our rhyme:
        What leaf-fring'd legend haunts about thy shape
          Of deities or mortals, or of both,
            In Tempe or the dales of Arcady?
              What men or gods are these? What maidens loth?
              What mad pursuit? What struggle to escape?
              What pipes and timbrels? What wild ecstasy?

Heard melodies are sweet, but those unheard
Are sweeter; therefore, ye soft pipes, play on;
  Not to the sensual ear, but, more endear'd,
    Pipe to the spirit ditties of no tone:
      Fair youth, beneath the trees, thou canst not leave

Thy song, nor ever can those trees be bare;
 Bold Lover, never, never canst thou kiss,
  Though winning near the goal yet, do not grieve;
   She cannot fade, though thou hast not thy bliss,
    For ever wilt thou love, and she be fair!

Ah, happy, happy boughs! that cannot shed
 Your leaves, nor ever bid the Spring adieu;
  And, happy melodist, unwearied,
   For ever piping songs for ever new;
    More happy love! more happy, happy love!
     For ever warm and still to be enjoy'd,
      For ever panting, and for ever young;
       All breathing human passion far above,
        That leaves a heart high-sorrowful and cloy'd,
         A burning forehead, and a parching tongue.

Who are these coming to the sacrifice?
 To what green altar, O mysterious priest,
  Lead'st thou that heifer lowing at the skies,
   And all her silken flanks with garlands drest?
    What little town by river or sea shore,
     Or mountain-built with peaceful citadel,
      Is emptied of this folk, this pious morn?
       And, little town, thy streets for evermore
        Will silent be; and not a soul to tell
         Why thou art desolate, can e'er return.

O Attic shape! Fair attitude! with brede
 Of marble men and maidens overwrought,
  With forest branches and the trodden weed;
   Thou, silent form, dost tease us out of thought
    As doth eternity: Cold Pastoral!
     When old age shall this generation waste,

Thou shalt remain, in midst of other woe
Than ours, a friend to man, to whom thou say'st,
"Beauty is truth, truth beauty,—that is all
Ye know on earth, and all ye need to know."

JOHN KEATS, Ode to a Grecian Urn (1819)

9.7   Let's read!

Season of mists and mellow fruitfulness,
Close bosom-friend of the maturing sun;
Conspiring with him how to load and bless
With fruit the vines that round the thatch-eaves run;
To bend with apples the mossed cottage-trees,
And fill all fruit with ripeness to the core;
To swell the gourd, and plump the hazel shells
With a sweet kernel; to set budding more,
And still more, later flowers for the bees,
Until they think warm days will never cease,
For Summer has o'er-brimmed their clammy cell.

Who hath not seen thee oft amid thy store?
Sometimes whoever seeks abroad may find
Thee sitting careless on a granary floor,
Thy hair soft-lifted by the winnowing wind;
Or on a half-reaped furrow sound asleep,
Drowsed with the fume of poppies, while thy hook
Spares the next swath and all its twined flowers;
And sometimes like a gleaner thou dost keep
Steady thy laden head across a brook;
Or by a cider-press, with patient look,
Thou watchest the last oozings, hours by hours.

Where are the songs of Spring? Ay, where are they?
 Think not of them, thou hast thy music too,—
 While barred clouds bloom the soft-dying day,
  And touch the stubble-plains with rosy hue;
   Then in a wailful choir, the small gnats mourn
   Among the river sallows, borne aloft
    Or sinking as the light wind lives or dies;
     And full-grown lambs loud bleat from hilly bourn;
     Hedge-crickets sing; and now with treble soft
     The redbreast whistles from a garden-croft,
      And gathering swallows twitter in the skies.

JOHN KEATS, Ode to Autumn (1820)

I SAT on cushioned otter-skin:
 My word was law from Ith to Emain,
 And shook at Inver Amergin
  The hearts of the world-troubling seamen,
  And drove tumult and war away
   From girl and boy and man and beast;
   The fields grew fatter day by day,
   The wild fowl of the air increased;
   And every ancient Ollave said,
    While he bent down his fading head.
    'He drives away the Northern cold.'
     They will not hush, the leaves a-flutter round me, the beech
leaves old.

I sat and mused and drank sweet wine;
 A herdsman came from inland valleys,
  Crying, the pirates drove his swine
   To fill their dark-beaked hollow galleys.
   I called my battle-breaking men

And my loud brazen battle-cars
 From rolling vale and rivery glen;
  And under the blinking of the stars
   Fell on the pirates by the deep,
    And hurled them in the gulph of sleep:
     These hands won many a torque of gold.
      They will not hush, the leaves a-flutter round me, the beech
leaves old.

But slowly, as I shouting slew
 And trampled in the bubbling mire,
  In my most secret spirit grew
   A whirling and a wandering fire:
    I stood: keen stars above me shone,
     Around me shone keen eyes of men:
      I laughed aloud and hurried on
       By rocky shore and rushy fen;
        I laughed because birds fluttered by,
         And starlight gleamed, and clouds flew high,
          And rushes waved and waters rolled.
           They will not hush, the leaves a-flutter round me, the beech
leaves old.

And now I wander in the woods
 When summer gluts the golden bees,
  Or in autumnal solitudes
   Arise the leopard-coloured trees;
    Or when along the wintry strands
     The cormorants shiver on their rocks;
      I wander on, and wave my hands,
       And sing, and shake my heavy locks.
        The grey wolf knows me; by one ear
         I lead along the woodland deer;
          The hares run by me growing bold.

They will not hush, the leaves a-flutter round me, the beech
leaves old.

I came upon a little town
 That slumbered in the harvest moon,
 And passed a-tiptoe up and down,
   Murmuring, to a fitful tune,
    How I have followed, night and day,
    A tramping of tremendous feet,
     And saw where this old tympan lay
      Deserted on a doorway seat,
       And bore it to the woods with me;
        Of some inhuman misery
         Our married voices wildly trolled.
          They will not hush, the leaves a-flutter round me, the beech
leaves old.

I sang how, when day's toil is done,
 Orchil shakes out her long dark hair
  That hides away the dying sun
   And sheds faint odours through the air:
    When my hand passed from wire to wire
    It quenched, with sound like falling dew
     The whirling and the wandering fire;
      But lift a mournful ulalu,
       For the kind wires are torn and still,
        And I must wander wood and hill
         Through summer's heat and winter's cold.
          They will not hush, the leaves a-flutter round me, the beech
leaves old.

W.B.YEATS, The Madness of King Goll (1928)

Behold her, single in the field,
 Yon solitary Highland Lass!
  Reaping and singing by herself;
   Stop here, or gently pass!
    Alone she cuts and binds the grain,
    And sings a melancholy strain;
     O listen! for the Vale profound
     Is overflowing with the sound.

No Nightingale did ever chaunt
 More welcome notes to weary bands
  Of travellers in some shady haunt,
   Among Arabian sands:
    A voice so thrilling ne'er was heard
     In spring-time from the Cuckoo-bird,
      Breaking the silence of the seas
      Among the farthest Hebrides.

Will no one tell me what she sings?—
 Perhaps the plaintive numbers flow
  For old, unhappy, far-off things,
   And battles long ago:
    Or is it some more humble lay,
     Familiar matter of to-day?
      Some natural sorrow, loss, or pain,
       That has been, and may be again?

Whate'er the theme, the Maiden sang
 As if her song could have no ending;
  I saw her singing at her work,
   And o'er the sickle bending;—
    I listened, motionless and still;
     And, as I mounted up the hill,
      The music in my heart I bore,

Long after it was heard no more.

WILLIAM WORDSWORTH, Solitary Reaper (1807)

A wind is ruffling the tawny pelt
 Of Africa. Kikuyu, quick as flies,
  Batten upon the bloodstreams of the veldt.
   Corpses are scattered through a paradise.
   Only the worm, colonel of carrion, cries:

"Waste no compassion on these separate dead!"
 Statistics justify and scholars seize
  The salients of colonial policy.
   What is that to the white child hacked in bed?
   To savages, expendable as Jews?

Threshed out by beaters, the long rushes break
 In a white dust of ibises whose cries
  Have wheeled since civilization's dawn
   From the parched river or beast-teeming plain.
    The violence of beast on beast is read
    As natural law, but upright man
    Seeks his divinity by inflicting pain.

Delirious as these worried beasts, his wars
 Dance to the tightened carcass of a drum,
  While he calls courage still that native dread
   Of the white peace contracted by the dead.
    Again brutish necessity wipes its hands
     Upon the napkin of a dirty cause, again
      A waste of our compassion, as with Spain,
      The gorilla wrestles with the superman.

I who am poisoned with the blood of both,
 Where shall I turn, divided to the vein?
  I who have cursed
    The drunken officer of British rule, how choose
      Between this Africa and the English tongue I love?
       Betray them both, or give back what they give?
        How can I face such slaughter and be cool?
        How can I turn from Africa and live?

                    WALCOTT, DEREK, A Far Cry from Africa (1962)

Go thou to Rome,—at once the Paradise,
 The grave, the city, and the wilderness;
  And where its wrecks like shattered mountains rise,
    And flowering weeds, and fragrant copses dress
     The bones of Desolation's nakedness
      Pass, till the spirit of the spot shall lead
        Thy footsteps to a slope of green access
         Where, like an infant's smile, over the dead
          A light of laughing flowers along the grass is spread;

And gray walls moulder round, on which dull Time
 Feeds, like slow fire upon a hoary brand;
  And one keen pyramid with wedge sublime,
    Pavilioning the dust of him who planned
     This refuge for his memory, doth stand
      Like flame transformed to marble; and beneath,
        A field is spread, on which a newer band
         Have pitched in Heaven's smile their camp of death,
          Welcoming him we lose with scarce extinguished breath.

Here pause: these graves are all too young as yet
 To have outgrown the sorrow which consigned
  Its charge to each; and if the seal is set,
    Here, on one fountain of a mourning mind,

Break it not thou! too surely shalt thou find
  Thine own well full, if thou returnest home,
    Of tears and gall. From the world's bitter wind
    Seek shelter in the shadow of the tomb.
      What Adonais is, why fear we to become?

The One remains, the many change and pass;
  Heaven's light forever shines, Earth's shadows fly;
   Life, like a dome of many-coloured glass,
    Stains the white radiance of Eternity,
      Until Death tramples it to fragments.—Die,
      If thou wouldst be with that which thou dost seek!
      Follow where all is fled!—Rome's azure sky,
        Flowers, ruins, statues, music, words, are weak
        The glory they transfuse with fitting truth to speak.

PERCY SHELLEY, ADONAIS

9.8   Snapshot

Cross rhymes are usual in longer stanzas and contribute to the rhythm of the poem, giving the poet room to avoid repetitions. In the ekphrastic poem, 'Ode to a Grecian Urn, John Keats focuses on this piece of art that he calls a historian. For the poet, the urn, an object that keeps the ashes of a body, encapsulates beauty and truth. Poetry encapsulates beauty but not always the truth.

Rhymes can be sophisticated and beautiful, but they can also be empty and artificial as its beauty should not be only in the form or in the melody, as he says, "Heard melodies are sweet, but those unheard/ Are sweeter; therefore, ye soft pipes, play on;" Poems are vessels that often carry implicit or enigmatic content. Thus, while poets work hard to adjust rhyme schemes and meter, they run the risk of privileging form and rules to the detriment of historical truths. The poem ends with the chiasmus that summarizes Keats' idea 'Beauty is truth, truth beauty – that is all/ Ye know on earth, and all ye need to know.'

9.9 Practice

It's your turn

Read the poems, identify the number of verses, stanzas and the rhyming pattern. In Wordsworth's poem "I Wandered as Cloud," the first three stanzas describe his experience and in the fourth stanza, the poet tells us how the experience opened his inward eye, giving him inspiration to write a poem. Derek Walcott in the first stanzas describe the suffering of Africans, but in the last stanza he positions himself and the way he feels by asking the question "How can I face such slaughter and be cool?" Now, it is your turn, select some of your poems and reorganize your stanzas.

9.10 Poets

Alexander Pope (1688 –1744)

was born in London. His father was a successful linen merchant. The poet's mother, Edith (1643–1733), was the daughter of William Turner, Esquire, of York. Both parents were Catholics. Pope's education was affected by the recently enacted Test Acts, which upheld the status of the established Church of England and banned Catholics from teaching, attending a university, voting, and holding public office on penalty of perpetual imprisonment. He then went on to two Roman Catholic schools in London. Such schools, though still illegal, were tolerated in some areas. Pope's most famous poem is The Rape of the Lock, first published in 1712, with a revised version in 1714.

Geoffrey Chaucer (1340 – 25 October)

was an English poet and author. Widely considered the greatest English poet of the Middle Ages, he is best known for The Canterbury Tales. He has been called the "father of English literature", or, alternatively, the "father of English poetry". He was the first writer to be buried in what has since come to be called Poets' Corner, in Westminster Abbey.He maintained a career in the civil service as a bureaucrat, courtier, diplomat, and member of parliament. The Canterbury Tales is a collection of 24 stories that runs to over 17,000 lines written in Middle English between 1387 and 1400. It is widely regarded as Chaucer's magnum opus. The tales (mostly written in verse, although some are in prose) are presented as part of a story-telling contest by a group of pilgrims as they travel together from London to Canterbury to visit the shrine of Saint Thomas Becket at Canterbury Cathedral. The prize for this contest is a free meal at the Tabard Inn at Southwark on their return. Among Chaucer's many other works are The Book of the Duchess, The House of Fame, The Legend of Good Women, and Troilus and Criseyde. He is seen as crucial in legitimizing the literary use of Middle English when the dominant literary languages in England were still French and Latin.

Percy Bysshe Shelley (1792 –1822)

was one of the major English Romantic poets. A radical in

his poetry as well as in his political and social views, Shelley did not achieve fame during his lifetime, but recognition of his achievements in poetry grew steadily following his death and he became an important influence on subsequent generations of poets including Robert Browning and W. B. Yeats. Among his best-known works are "Ozymandias" (1818), "Ode to the West Wind" (1819), "To a Skylark" (1820), and Adonais (1821) and Prometheus Unbound (1820).

Reference

Kierkegaard, S. "Either/Or." In the Essential Kierkegaard. Edited by Howard Hong and Edna Hong. New Jersey: Princeton University Press, 2000.

Chapter 10

IMAGERY

> If there can be a better way for the real world to
> include the one of images, it will require an ecology
> not only of real things but of images well.

Susan Sontag, On Photography

IMAGERY refers to the images produced in the mind by language, leading the reader to physical perception. This chapter focuses on how simile, metaphor, and synesthesia connect images to imagination to express feelings that represent human experience.

Poets imagine implicit connections among opposing and dissimilar objects, ideas, and structures, challenging the lexical and creating new meanings. Imagination dislocates meaning to create images that are more appropriate to express the poet's ideas, as Paul Ricoeur states,

> "metaphor is living by virtue of the fact that it introduces
> the spark of imagination into thinking." (358)

10.1   Simile

Similes are explicit comparisons between two objects or ideas connected with 'as' or 'like, as in "you are sweet as a sugar plum." In the poem, 'There is no Frigate like a Book,' Emily Dickinson places reading and literature at the center of the poem, drawing clear comparisons between poetry and life, thus transposing the reader to an imaginary world.

> Example:
> There is no Frigate like a Book
> To take us Lands away
>
> **EMILY DICKINSON**, There is no frigate like a book (1894)

10.2   Metaphor

A metaphor is an implicit comparison in which one idea or an object replaces another. It always works well because images are part of our way of constructing ideas, and we usually use images to make a comparison in everyday speech. It is usual to hear 'time is money,' 'it is raining cats and dogs,' or 'you are my sunshine.'

In poetry, metaphors are one of the most basic tools to escape the common language. Through unexpected comparisons, poets invite readers to use their imagination, as in the short poem below,

> Example:
>   Fame is a bee.
>   It has a song—
>   It has a sting—
>   Ah, too, it has a wing.

> **EMILY DICKINSON**, Fame is a bee (1898)

The poet compares fame to a bee, saying it is dangerous as it has a sting and a wing. Dickinson says that fame is ephemeral and may hurt. Metaphors go far beyond literal meanings and open up ways of expressing sensory and physical perceptions. Through images, poets convey layers of meaning to a concrete object, an action, or an idea, inviting the reader to feel something instead of understanding exactly what the poet wants to express.

Metaphors usually appear silently, without calling attention to any explicit comparison. In Dickinson's poem "I Dwell in Possibility," the poet says that prose is not a fair house, as it does not give her doors and windows, symbolizing the freedom she needs to create.

> Example:
>   I dwell in Possibility –
>   A fairer House than Prose –
>   More numerous of Windows –
>   Superior – for Doors –
>
>   Of Chambers as the Cedars –
>   Impregnable of eye –
>   And for an everlasting Roof
>   The Gambrels of the Sky –

Of Visitors – the fairest –
For Occupation – This –
The spreading wide my narrow Hands
To gather Paradise –

EMILY DICKINSON, I Dwell in Possibility (1894)

In poetry, powerful images emerge from opposing objects and ideas that out of the context would not suggest any meaning, such as "hope and feathers." Dickinson does not mention straight away that hope is a bird, or that hope can fly, but she gives more substance to the metaphor by giving the reader space to ask questions about the meanings of hope, faith, and soul. Why does a soul need hope? What does a hopeless soul mean? Why do humans need to have faith?

Example:
Hope is the thing with feathers -
That perches in the soul -
And sings the tune without the words -
And never stops - at all -

And sweetest - in the Gale - is heard -
And sore must be the storm -
That could abash the little Bird
That kept so many warm -

I've heard it in the chillest land -
And on the strangest Sea -
Yet - never - in Extremity,
It asked a crumb - of me.

EMILY DICKINSON, Hope is the thing with feathers (1894)

10.3 Synesthesia

Synesthesia is a condition in which the stimulation of one sense causes unusual experiences in a different sense. It is not a disorder, but a biological condition found in a minority of people. The term comes from the Greek word Syn that means together and aesthesis, meaning perception. For people with synesthesia, words can have taste; names can have color, and a specific sequence of numbers may dance through space. For example, the sound of a saxophone may have a sweet taste, or the letter A can be the color red. Imagine someone who sees a tree and feels like tasting an apple.

Vision and color is by far the most common synesthetic experience relative to touch, taste, and hearing. However, there are many types of synesthesia, such as names that have taste, for example, Sophia could taste grapes and Ana oranges. Synesthetic perceptions are specific to each person. If someone observes a particular letter, for example, the letter B, and sees the color blue around it, another synesthetic person may see the same letter in a different color, such as green or red. It means that synesthesia causes different feelings and perceptions in those who have the same condition. Synesthesia can be involuntary, projected, generic, or emotional.

Involuntary – People who have synesthesia do not have control of the feelings caused by synesthesia

Projected – People project synesthetic perception outside their bodies. They see images, colors, and objects.

Generic – The perception is the same every time a person has the same experience. For example, if the person listens to a particular song by Justin Bieber, he/she tastes cod oil.

Emotional – Synesthetic perceptions cause emotional re-actions as a feeling of pleasure, anger, or fear, depending on the experience.

Synesthesia and poetry

In poetry, a synesthetic metaphor appears as a blending or confusion of different senses, such as smell, sight, hearing, taste, touch, in which one sense always refers to another one. An example is a reference or description of some colors in an environment as loud or warm. In describing one sense using another sense, the poet creates metaphors and similes, as in the examples,

Example:
 When there was heard a sound, so loud, it shook
 The towers amid the moonlight, yet more sweet
 Than any voice but thine, sweetest of all;
 A long, long sound, as it would never end;
 And all the inhabitants leapt suddenly
 Out of their rest, and gathered in the streets,
 Looking in wonder up to Heaven, while yet
 The music pealed along . . .

PERCY SHELLEY, Prometheus Unbound, III 54-60 (1820)

Example:
 Heard melodies are sweet, but those unheard
 Are sweeter; therefore, ye soft pipes, play on;

JOHN KEATS, Ode to a Grecian Urn (1819)

Example:
 I rise as from a bath of sparkling water,
 A bath of azure light, among dark rocks,
 Out of the stream of sound.

   PERCY SHELLEY, Prometheus Unbound III 503-5 (1820)

Example:
 And never will we part, till thy chaste sister,
 Who guides the frozen and inconstant moon,
 Will look on thy more warm and equal light
 Till her heart thaw like flakes of April snow,
 And love thee.

   PERCY SHELLEY, Prometheus Unbound, III 85-89 (1820)

In the examples we observe how poets dwell on sensory impressions. In some verses, synesthesia is more obvious as in the words 'heard' and 'sweet' in Keats' poem, a blending of taste and hearing. In other poems, as in Shelley's "Prometheus Unbound," synesthetic metaphors are more unpredictable as in the words 'sparkling water' bath of azure light,' and 'stream of sound' that create intense images with the fusion of colors and sounds. Romantic poets, such as John Keats and Percy Shelley followed the rule of hierarchy. For them, lower senses such as touch, smell, and taste contain less vocabulary to describe images, while higher senses as sight, and hearing provide more vocabulary. Considering that most humans use higher senses to understand the world, they are the primary sensory input in everyday life as well as in poetry.

10.4   Let's read!

There is no Frigate like a Book
 To take us Lands away
  Nor any Coursers like a Page
   Of prancing Poetry —
    This Traverse may the poorest take
     Without oppress of Toll —
      How frugal is the Chariot
       That bears the Human Soul —

EMILY DICKINSON, There is no Frigate like a book (1894)

O pencil,
 A friend to me,
  With you, I create a universe once more,
   With you, I create things that aren't real,
    I give life to words which can't move,
     And I create places where the laws of nature are disobeyed.
      You pencil, do I have complete power over you,
       Or do you fly out of my hand,
        And write what you want?
         You pencil,
          A divine instrument,
           You have the ability to jump out of my hand,
            Creating worlds invisible to the human eye!

ALLAN BISHOP, To my little friend (2018)

Rudolph Reed was oaken.
 His wife was oaken too.
  And his two good girls and his good little man
   Oakened as they grew.

I am not hungry for berries.
I am not hungry for bread.
But hungry hungry for a house
Where at night a man in bed

May never hear the plaster
Stir as if in pain.
May never hear the roaches
Falling like fat rain.

Where never wife and children need
Go blinking through the gloom.
Where every room of many rooms
Will be full of room.

Oh my home may have its east or west
Or north or south behind it.
All I know is I shall know it,
And fight for it when I find it.

It was in a street of bitter white
That he made his application.
For Rudolph Reed was oakener
Than others in the nation.

The agent's steep and steady stare
Corroded to a grin.
Why, you black old, tough old hell of a man,
Move your family in!

Nary a grin grinned Rudolph Reed,
Nary a curse cursed he,
But moved in his House. With his dark little wife,

And his dark little children three.

A neighbor would *look*, with a yawning eye
  That squeezed into a slit.
   But the Rudolph Reeds and the children three
    Were too joyous to notice it.

For were they not firm in a home of their own
  With windows everywhere
   And a beautiful banistered stair
    And a front yard for flowers and a back yard for grass?

The first night, a rock, big as two fists.
  The second, a rock big as three.
   But nary a curse cursed Rudolph Reed.
    (Though oaken as man could be.)

The third night, a silvery ring of glass.
  Patience ached to endure.
   But he looked, and lo! small Mabel's blood
    Was staining her gaze so pure.

Then up did rise our Rudolph Reed
  And pressed the hand of his wife,
   And went to the door with a thirty-four
    And a beastly butcher knife.

He ran like a mad thing into the night.
  And the words in his mouth were stinking.
   By the time he had hurt his first white man
    He was no longer thinking.

   ...

Small Mabel whimpered all night long,
  For calling herself the cause.
   Her oak-eyed mother did no thing
    But change the bloody gauze.

  GWENDOLYN BROOKS, The Ballad of Rudolph Reed (1963)

Mark but this flea, and mark in this,
  How little that which thou deniest me is;
   It sucked me first, and now sucks thee,
    And in this flea our two bloods mingled be;
     Thou know'st that this cannot be said
      A sin, nor shame, nor loss of maidenhead,
       Yet this enjoys before it woo,
        And pampered swells with one blood made of two,
        And this, alas, is more than we would do.

Oh stay, three lives in one flea spare,
  Where we almost, nay more than married are.
   This flea is you and I, and this
    Our marriage bed, and marriage temple is;
     Though parents grudge, and you, w'are met,
      And cloistered in these living walls of jet.
       Though use make you apt to kill me,
        Let not to that, self-murder added be,
         And sacrilege, three sins in killing three.

Cruel and sudden, hast thou since
  Purpled thy nail, in blood of innocence?
   Wherein could this flea guilty be,
    Except in that drop which it sucked from thee?
     Yet thou triumph'st, and say'st that thou
      Find'st not thy self, nor me the weaker now;

'Tis true; then learn how false, fears be:
  Just so much honor, when thou yield'st to me,
  Will waste, as this flea's death took life

JOHN DONNE, The Flea (1633)

The sky is cloudy, yellowed by the smoke.
For view there are the houses opposite
Cutting the sky with one long line of wall
Like solid fog: far as the eye can stretch
Monotony of surface & of form
Without a break to hang a guess upon.
No bird can make a shadow as it flies,
For all is shadow, as in ways o'erhung
By thickest canvass, where the golden rays
Are clothed in hemp. No figure lingering
Pauses to feed the hunger of the eye
Or rest a little on the lap of life.
All hurry on & look upon the ground,
Or glance unmarking at the passers by
The wheels are hurrying too, cabs, carriages
All closed, in multiplied identity.
The world seems one huge prison-house & court
Where men are punished at the slightest cost,
With lowest rate of colour, warmth & joy.

GEORGE ELIOT, In a London Drawing Room (1870)

AH, London! London! our delight,
  Great flower that opens but at night,

Great City of the midnight sun,
  Whose day begins when day is done.

Lamp after lamp against the sky
  Opens a sudden beaming eye,
    Leaping alight on either hand,
      The iron lilies of the Strand.

Like dragonflies, the hansoms hover,
  With jeweled eyes, to catch the lover;
    The streets are full of lights and loves,
      Soft gowns, and flutter of soiled doves.

The human moths about the light
  Dash and cling close in dazed delight,
    And burn and laugh, the world and wife,
      For this is London, this is life!

Upon thy petals butterflies,
  But at thy root, some say, there lies,
    A world of weeping trodden things,
      Poor worms that have not eyes or wings.

From out corruption of their woe
  Springs this bright flower that charms us so,
    Men die and rot deep out of sight
      To keep this jungle-flower bright.

Paris and London, World-Flowers twain
  Wherewith the World-Tree blooms again,
    Since Time hath gathered Babylon,
      And withered Rome still withers on.

Sidon and Tyre were such as ye,
  How bright they shone upon the tree!
    But Time hath gathered, both are gone,
    And no man sails to Babylon.

RICHARD LE GALLIENNE, A ballad of London (1892)

Fame is a bee.
  It has a song—
  It has a sting—
    Ah, too, it has a wing.

EMILY DICKINSON, Fame is a bee (1763)

Fame is a fickle food
  Upon a shifting plate
  Whose table once a
    Guest but not
      The second time is set
        Whose crumbs the crows inspect
          And with ironic caw
            Flap past it to the
              Farmer's corn
                Men eat of it and die

EMILY DICKINSON, Fame is a fickle food (1890)

We wear the mask that grins and lies,
  It hides our cheeks and shades our eyes,—
    This debt we pay to human guile;

With torn and bleeding hearts we smile,
And mouth with myriad subtleties.

Why should the world be overwise,
In counting all our tears and sighs?
Nay, let them only see us, while
We wear the mask.

We smile, but, O great Christ, our cries
To thee from tortured souls arise.
We sing, but oh the clay is vile
Beneath our feet, and long the mile;
But let the world dream otherwise,
We wear the mask!

PAUL LAWRENCE DUNBAR, We wear the mask (1895)

Well, son, I'll tell you:
Life for me ain't been no crystal stair.
It's had tacks in it,
And splinters,
And boards torn up,
And places with no carpet on the floor—
Bare.
But all the time
I'se been a-climbin' on,
And reachin' landin's,
And turnin' corners,
And sometimes goin' in the dark
Where there ain't been no light.
So boy, don't you turn back.
Don't you set down on the steps
'Cause you finds it's kinder hard.

Don't you fall now—
For I'se still goin', honey,
I'se still climbin',
And life for me ain't been no crystal stair.

LANGSTON HUGHES, Mother to son (1922)

Well, my path lately lay through a great city
Into the woody hills surrounding it;
A sentinel was sleeping at the gate;
When there was heard a sound, so loud, it shook
The towers amid the moonlight, yet more sweet
Than any voice but thine, sweetest of all;
A long, long sound, as it would never end;
And all the inhabitants leapt suddenly
Out of their rest, and gathered in the streets,
...
After some foul disguise had fallen, and all
Were somewhat changed, and after brief surprise
And greetings of delighted wonder, all
Went to their sleep again; and when the dawn
Came, wouldst thou think that toads, and snakes, and efts,
Could e'er be beautiful? yet so they were,
And that with little change of shape or hue;
All things had put their evil nature off;
I cannot tell my joy, when o'er a lake,
Upon a drooping bough with nightshade twined,
I saw two azure halcyons clinging downward
And thinning one bright bunch of amber berries,
With quick long beaks, and in the deep there lay
Those lovely forms imaged as in a sky;
So with my thoughts full of these happy changes,

We meet again, the happiest change of all.

      PERCY SHELLEY, Prometheus Unbound III 50-85 (1820)

One evening (surely I was led by her)
I went alone into a Shepherd's Boat,
A Skiff that to a Willow tree was tied
Within a rocky Cave, its usual home.
'Twas by the shores of Patterdale, a Vale
Wherein I was a Stranger, thither come
A School-boy Traveller, at the Holidays.
Forth rambled from the Village Inn alone
No sooner had I sight of this small Skiff,
Discover'd thus by unexpected chance,
Than I unloos'd her tether and embark'd.
The moon was up, the Lake was shining clear
Among the hoary mountains; from the Shore
I push'd, and struck the oars and struck again
In cadence, and my little Boat mov'd on
Even like a Man who walks with stately step
Though bent on speed. It was an act of stealth
And troubled pleasure; not without the voice
Of mountain-echoes did my Boat move on,
Leaving behind her still on either side
Small circles glittering idly in the moon,
Until they melted all into one track
Of sparkling light. A rocky Steep uprose

Above the Cavern of the Willow tree
And now, as suited one who proudly row'd
With his best skill, I fix'd a steady view
Upon the top of that same craggy ridge,
The bound of the horizon, for behind

Was nothing but the stars and the grey sky.

WILLIAM WORDSWORTH, from The Prelude

10.5   Snapshot

Imagining means to have a mental picture of something, and display it in a depicting mode, revealing the objects' most illuminating facets and producing similarities that do not exist. As similarities are only produced by imagination, a metaphor is generated in the borderline between verbal and non-verbal, truth and untruth, and if images can reconstruct reality, a metaphor may be seen as a model for changing our way of looking at things and perceiving the world. Nevertheless, the poetic language suggests and reveals the deep structures of the phenomenon, an object, a fact, a situation, to which humans relate.

Gwendolyn Brooks' poem narrates the story of a black man who, in search of a better life, moves to a bitter white neighborhood. The first metaphor in the poem is 'Rudolph Reed was oaken,' and in the following verses, the reader discovers that his wife and children were oaken too. The poet compares the family to the strength of wood, an oak tree. The following image is 'hungry hungry for a house.' Rudolph Reed says he does not need 'berries' or 'bread;' he strives for dignity.

The image of oak appears again, as he finds a house 'in a street of bitter white' because 'Rudolph Reed was oakener/ Than the others in the nation.' The poet includes the simile 'a rock, big as two fists,' foreshadowing the physical violence that happens after the third night when a rock breaks the glass of the window and targets his daughter. A synesthetic image appears at the end of the poem 'And the words of his mouth were stinking,' a blending of smell and sound, which rhymes with 'thinking' in the verse 'He was no longer thinking,' unveiling the state of the mind of a man who found in madness a refuge.

In the poem, 'Mother to Son,' Langston Hughes represents the struggle of African Americans to overcome disillusion in a world where everything appears to be torn. The mother teaches her son about strength and resilience by stating that life has not been a crystal stair. For this metaphor, the reader can imagine a myriad of images such as transparency and fairness. Images of splinters and stacks found in the stair seem to push the mother to the opposite way in this constant struggle to survive. The absence of light connected to fear is an image that children understand well but it is in the darkness that the son will have to find the strength to keep walking.

10.6 Practice

It's your turn

Read carefully all poems you wrote so far and refine your metaphors.

10.7 Poets

Paul Laurence Dunbar (1872 - 1906)
was an American poet, novelist and playwright. He was married to Alice Dunbar. Among his works are *On the River* and *Majors and Minors*.

John Donne (1572 - 1631)

was a poet and cleric of the Church of England. Some of his poems were considered inappropriate to a religious man because of metaphors relating to sexuality. One of his most famous and controversial poems is The Flea.

Langston Hughes (1902- 1967)

was an African American poet, social activist, columnist, novelist and playwright. He was one of the innovators of the literary form called jazz poetry. One of the leaders of the Harlem renaissance, his poems revealed not only the rhythm of jazz but also the social conditions of the African American population. Among his most famous poems are "Mother to Son, Dreams," "The Dream Keeper," "The Juke Box Love Song" and "The Blues."

Reference

Sontag, Susan. On Photography, Picador: New York, 1973.

Ricoeur, Paul. The Rule of Metaphor. The Creation of Meaning in Language. Routledge: London and New York, 1986.

Chapter 11

SOUND AND RHYTHM

> ... transform reality into something beautiful
> derives from its relative weakness as a means of
> conveying the truth ...

> Susan Sontag, On Photography

SOUND effects can be one of the most captivating aspects of poetry. Melody always engages readers, bringing rhythm and movement to the poem. It is worth noting that repetition of sounds, words and sentences can substitute rhyme and meter, as melody involves and causes enchantment. However, poets should never abuse of sound devices but always follow the rhythm of natural speech. In this chapter, let's see how alliteration, anaphora, and onomatopoeia can capture the ear and the heart.

11.1 Alliteration

Alliteration is the repetition of initial consonant sounds in two or more neighboring words. It contributes to certain forms of meaning, for example, the repetition /s/ sounds may suggest whispering or snake sounds. Suppose the poet wants to suggest danger, intrigues, and fake moves, the repetition of /s/ can produce this effect. In Dickinson's poem, as she reveals that the worm transformed into a snake, the stanza brings the words **slim/secreted/swim** alliterate.

Example:
 Then to a Rhythm Slim
 Secreted in his Form
 As Patterns swim
 Projected him.

EMILY DICKINSON, In Winter in my room' (1914)

The use of alliteration often helps the reader to be more involved with the rhythm and memorize the poem. Everybody who reads Macbeth remembers the witches saying

Example:
 Fair is foul, foul is fair.

WILLIAM SHAKESPEARE, Macbeth (1606)

Alliteration can create an idea that something is about to happen, so the pace of the verses tells the reader that something is going faster and faster. It gives a good sense of rhythm and but poets should not abuse the repetition of sounds. Alliteration should never be included in the whole poem, as it runs the risk of making it artificial. Observe how Dickinson uses repetition of /l/ sound 'love' and 'life' to give rhythm to verse and emphasize the idea of the everlasting nature of love.

Example:
Love is anterior to Life —
Posterior to Death
Initial of Creation, and
The Exponent of Earth

EMILY DICKINSON, Love is anterior to Life (1896)

11.2   Anaphora

Anaphora is the repetition of one or more words at the beginning of several successive sentences. Anaphora may have a spell effect, some kind of incantatory melody caused by repetition as if the reader is taken somewhere unconsciously. Religious poetry always uses anaphora, as Psalm 136.

Example:
Give thanks to the Lord of lords:
His love endures forever.
to him who alone does great wonders,
His love endures forever.
who by his understanding made the heavens,
His love endures forever.
who spread out the earth upon the waters,
His love endures forever.
who made the great lights—
His love endures forever.
the sun to govern the day,

His love endures forever.
the moon and stars to govern the night;
His love endures forever.

PSALM 136 V. 3-9, Bible

The psalm reminds us the everlasting love of God by high-lighting God's creation. Observe how the poet repeats "who" referring to God in the sentences: " who by his understanding made the heavens/ who made the great lights—/ who spread out the earth upon the waters. Repetitions do not have any connections with metrics, the number of syllables of a verse, or rhymes. Poets find creative ways to incorporate anaphora. It can appear in the whole poem or in one stanza as in Blake's Jerusalem, or in one line of a longer stanza, as in Dickinson's 'I would not paint a picture.'

Example:
  Bring me my Bow of burning gold:
  Bring me my arrows of desire:
  Bring me my Spear: O clouds unfold!
  Bring me my Chariot of fire!

WILLIAM BLAKE, Jerusalem (1794)

Example:
  I would not paint — a picture —
  I'd rather be the One
  It's bright impossibility
  To dwell — delicious — on —

And wonder how the fingers feel
Whose rare — celestial — stir —
Evokes so sweet a torment —
Such sumptuous — Despair —

I would not talk, like Cornets —
I'd rather be the One
Raised softly to the Ceilings —
And out, and easy on —

EMILY DICKINSON, I would not paint a picture (1892)

11.3   Consonance

Consonance is the correspondence or resemblance of consonant sounds. It does not have to be at the beginning of the sentence, as pink and lank in the example,

Example:
 I came upon a Worm—
Pink, lank and warm—
But as he was a worm

EMILY DICKINSON, In Winter in my room (1914)

11.4   Assonance

It is a correspondence of vowel sounds across a poetic line or a poem, as in 'deeper' and 'sea,' as in this verse,

Example:
The Brain is deeper than the sea –

EMILY DICKINSON, The Brain is wider than the Sky (1896)

11.5   Onomatopoeia

It describes the sound a thing or an action evokes, for example, hiss, buzz, crack, and so forth. Poets use onomatopoeia to replicate sounds things, actions, and situations, producing sound effects.

Example:
I heard a Fly buzz - when I died -
The Stillness in the Room
Was like the Stillness in the Air -
Between the Heaves of Storm –

EMILY DICKINSON, I heard a Fly buzz when I died' (1896)

11.6   Let's read!

The gray sea and the long black land;
  And the yellow half-moon large and low;
  And the startled little waves that leap
   In fiery ringlets from their sleep,
    As I gain the coving with pushing prow,
    And quench its speed in the slushy sand

Then a mile of warm sea-scented beach;
 Three fields to cross till a farm appears;
  A tap at the pane, the quick sharp scratch
  And blue spurt of a lighted match,
   And a voice less loud, thro' its joys and fears,
    Than the two hearts beating each to each!

                    ROBERT BROWNING, Meeting at Night (1845)

And did those feet in ancient time
 Walk upon Englands mountains green:
 And was the holy Lamb of God,
  On Englands pleasant pastures seen?

And did the Countenance Divine,
 Shine forth upon our clouded hills?
 And was Jerusalem builded here,
  Among these dark Satanic Mills?

Bring me my Bow of burning gold:
 Bring me my arrows of desire:
  Bring me my Spear: O clouds unfold!
  Bring me my Chariot of fire!

I will not cease from Mental Fight,
 Nor shall my sword sleep in my hand:
 Till we have built Jerusalem,
  In Englands green & pleasant Land.

                    WILLIAM BLAKE, Jerusalem (1794)

Eyes that last I saw in tears
 Through division
  Here in death's dream kingdom
   The golden vision reappears
    I see the eyes but not the tears
     This is my affliction

This is my affliction
 Eyes I shall not see again
  Eyes of decision
   Eyes I shall not see unless
    At the door of death's other kingdom
     Where, as in this,
      The eyes outlast a little while
       A little while outlast the tears
        And hold us in derision.

T.S.ELIOT, Eyes that last I saw in tears (1919)

When I heard the learn'd astronomer,
 When the proofs, the figures, were ranged in columns
  before me,
   When I was shown the charts and diagrams, to add, divide,
    and measure them,
     When I sitting heard the astronomer where he lectured
      with much applause in the lecture-room,
       How soon unaccountable I became tired and sick,
        Till rising and gliding out I wander'd off by myself,
         In the mystical moist night-air, and from time to time,
          Look'd up in perfect silence at the stars.

WALT WHITMAN, When I heard the learned Astronomer (1865)

O generation of the thoroughly smug
  and thoroughly uncomfortable,
   I have seen fishermen picnicking in the sun,
    I have seen them with untidy families,
     I have seen their smiles full of teeth
      and heard ungainly laughter.
       And I am happier than you are,
        And they were happier than I am;
         And the fish swim in the lake
          and do not even own clothing.

                    EZRA POUND, Salutation

the Harlem night
 and wrap around you,
  Take the neon lights and make a crown,
   Take the Lenox Avenue busses,
    Taxis, subways,
     And for your love song tone their rumble down.
      Take Harlem's heartbeat,
       Make a drumbeat,
        Put it on a record, let it whirl,
         And while we listen to it play,
          Dance with you till day—
           Dance with you, my sweet brown Harlem girl

            LANGSTON HUGHES, Juke Box love Song (1922)

It SHUSHES
 It hushes
  The loudness in the road.
   It flitter-twitters,
    And laughs away from me.
     It laughs a lovely whiteness,

And whitely whirls away,
  To be
   Some otherwhere,
    Still white as milk or shirts,
     So beautiful it hurts.

                    GWENDOLYN BROOKS, Cynthia in the snow

I would not paint — a picture —
 I'd rather be the One
  It's bright impossibility
   To dwell — delicious — on —
    And wonder how the fingers feel
     Whose rare — celestial — stir —
      Evokes so sweet a torment —
       Such sumptuous — Despair —

I would not talk, like Cornets —
 I'd rather be the One
  Raised softly to the Ceilings —
   And out, and easy on —
    Through Villages of Ether —
     Myself endued Balloon
      By but a lip of Metal —
       The pier to my Pontoon —

Nor would I be a Poet —
 It's finer — Own the Ear —
  Enamored — impotent — content —
   The License to revere,
    A privilege so awful
     What would the Dower be,
      Had I the Art to stun myself

With Bolts — of Melody!

EMILY DICKINSON, I would not paint a picture (1892)

In Winter in my Room
I came upon a Worm—
Pink, lank and warm—
But as he was a worm
And worms presume
Not quite with him at home—
Secured him by a string
To something neighboring
And went along.

A Trifle afterward
A thing occurred
I'd not believe it if I heard
But state with creeping blood—
A snake with mottles rare
Surveyed my chamber floor
In feature as the worm before
But ringed with power—

The very string with which
I tied him—too
When he was mean and new
That string was there—

I shrank—"How fair you are"!
Propitiation's claw—
"Afraid," he hissed
"Of me"?

"No cordiality" —
He fathomed me—
  Then to a Rhythm Slim
  Secreted in his Form
  As Patterns swim
  Projected him.

That time I flew
 Both eyes his way
  Lest he pursue
  Nor ever ceased to run
  Till in a distant Town
  Towns on from mine
  I set me down
  This was a dream.

         EMILY DICKINSON, In Winter in my room (1914)

I heard a Fly buzz - when I died -
The Stillness in the Room
 Was like the Stillness in the Air -
 Between the Heaves of Storm -

The Eyes around - had wrung them dry -
And Breaths were gathering firm
 For that last Onset - when the King
 Be witnessed - in the Room -

I willed my Keepsakes - Signed away
 What portion of me be
 Assignable - and then it was
 There interposed a Fly -

With Blue - uncertain - stumbling Buzz -
  Between the light - and me -
  And then the Windows failed - and then
    I could not see to see -

     EMILY DICKINSON, I Heard a fly buzz when I died (1896)

Let us go then, you and I,
  When the evening is spread out against the sky
  Like a patient etherized upon a table;
    Let us go, through certain half-deserted streets,
      The muttering retreats
        Of restless nights in one-night cheap hotels
        And sawdust restaurants with oyster-shells:
          Streets that follow like a tedious argument
            Of insidious intent
              To lead you to an overwhelming question ...
            Oh, do not ask, "What is it?"
            Let us go and make our visit.

In the room the women come and go
  Talking of Michelangelo.

The yellow fog that rubs its back upon the window-panes,
  The yellow smoke that rubs its muzzle on the window-panes,
    Licked its tongue into the corners of the evening,
      Lingered upon the pools that stand in drains,
        Let fall upon its back the soot that falls from chimneys,
          Slipped by the terrace, made a sudden leap,
            And seeing that it was a soft October night,
              Curled once about the house, and fell asleep.

And indeed there will be time
 For the yellow smoke that slides along the street,
  Rubbing its back upon the window-panes;
   There will be time, there will be time
    To prepare a face to meet the faces that you meet;
   There will be time to murder and create,
    And time for all the works and days of hands
     That lift and drop a question on your plate;
    Time for you and time for me,
     And time yet for a hundred indecisions,
     And for a hundred visions and revisions,
      Before the taking of a toast and tea.

In the room the women come and go
 Talking of Michelangelo.

And indeed there will be time
 To wonder, "Do I dare?" and, "Do I dare?"
  Time to turn back and descend the stair,
   With a bald spot in the middle of my hair —
    (They will say: "How his hair is growing thin!")
     My morning coat, my collar mounting firmly to the chin,
      My necktie rich and modest, but asserted by a simple pin —
     (They will say: "But how his arms and legs are thin!")
      Do I dare
       Disturb the universe?
       In a minute there is time
        For decisions and revisions which a minute will reverse.

For I have known them all already, known them all:
 Have known the evenings, mornings, afternoons,
  I have measured out my life with coffee spoons;
   I know the voices dying with a dying fall
    Beneath the music from a farther room.

So how should I presume?

And I have known the eyes already, known them all— The eyes that
fix you in a formulated phrase,
  And when I am formulated, sprawling on a pin,
  When I am pinned and wriggling on the wall,
   Then how should I begin
    To spit out all the butt-ends of my days and ways?
    And how should I presume?

And I have known the arms already, known them all—
Arms that are braceleted and white and bare
(But in the lamplight, downed with light brown hair!)
  Is it perfume from a dress
   That makes me so digress?
    Arms that lie along a table, or wrap about a shawl.
    And should I then presume?
    And how should I begin?

Shall I say, I have gone at dusk through narrow streets
And watched the smoke that rises from the pipes
  Of lonely men in shirt-sleeves, leaning out of windows? ...

I should have been a pair of ragged claws
Scuttling across the floors of silent seas.

And the afternoon, the evening, sleeps so peacefully!
Smoothed by long fingers,
  Asleep ... tired ... or it malingers,
   Stretched on the floor, here beside you and me.
   Should I, after tea and cakes and ices,
    Have the strength to force the moment to its crisis?
    But though I have wept and fasted, wept and prayed,

Though I have seen my head (grown slightly bald) brought in
upon a platter,
I am no prophet — and here's no great matter;
I have seen the moment of my greatness flicker,
And I have seen the eternal Footman hold my coat, and
snicker,
And in short, I was afraid.

And would it have been worth it, after all,
After the cups, the marmalade, the tea,
Among the porcelain, among some talk of you and me,
Would it have been worth while,
To have bitten off the matter with a smile,
To have squeezed the universe into a ball
To roll it towards some overwhelming question,
To say: "I am Lazarus, come from the dead,
Come back to tell you all, I shall tell you all" —
If one, settling a pillow by her head
Should say: "That is not what I meant at all;
That is not it, at all."

And would it have been worth it, after all,
Would it have been worth while,
After the sunsets and the dooryards and the sprinkled streets,
After the novels, after the teacups, after the skirts that trail along
the floor—
And this, and so much more?—
It is impossible to say just what I mean!
But as if a magic lantern threw the nerves in patterns on a
screen:
Would it have been worth while
If one, settling a pillow or throwing off a shawl,
And turning toward the window, should say:
"That is not it at all,

That is not what I meant, at all."

No! I am not Prince Hamlet, nor was meant to be;
Am an attendant lord, one that will do
To swell a progress, start a scene or two,
Advise the prince; no doubt, an easy tool,
Deferential, glad to be of use,
Politic, cautious, and meticulous;
Full of high sentence, but a bit obtuse;
At times, indeed, almost ridiculous—
Almost, at times, the Fool.

I grow old ... I grow old ...
I shall wear the bottoms of my trousers rolled.

Shall I part my hair behind? Do I dare to eat a peach?
I shall wear white flannel trousers, and walk upon the beach.
I have heard the mermaids singing, each to each.

I do not think that they will sing to me.

I have seen them riding seaward on the waves
Combing the white hair of the waves blown back
When the wind blows the water white and black.
We have lingered in the chambers of the sea
By sea-girls wreathed with seaweed red and brown
Till human voices wake us ...

T. S. ELIOT, The Song of Alfred Prufrock (1915)

Hold fast to dreams
For if dreams die

Life is a broken-winged bird
That cannot fly.
Hold fast to dreams
For when dreams go
Life is a barren field
Frozen with snow.

LANGSTON HUGHES, Dreams (1922)

What are you able to build with your blocks?
Castles and palaces, temples and docks.
Rain may keep raining, and others go roam,
But I can be happy and building at home.

Let the sofa be mountains, the carpet be sea,
There I'll establish a city for me:
A kirk and a mill and a palace beside,
And a harbor as well where my vessels may ride.

Great is the palace with pillar and wall,
A sort of a tower on top of it all,
And steps coming down in an orderly way
To where my toy vessels lie safe in the bay.

This one is sailing and that one is moored:
Hark to the song of the sailors on board!
And see on the steps of my palace, the kings
Coming and going with presents and things!

ROBERT LOUIS STEVENSON, Block City (1885

For those of us who live at the shoreline

standing upon the constant edges of decision
 crucial and alone
  for those of us who cannot indulge
   the passing dreams of choice
    who love in doorways coming and going
     in the hours between dawns
      looking inward and outward
       at once before and after
        seeking a now that can breed
         futures
          ...

       For those of us
        who were imprinted with fear
         like a faint line in the center of our foreheads
         learning to be afraid with our mother's milk
         for by this weapon
          this illusion of some safety to be found
           the heavy-footed hoped to silence us
            For all of us
             this instant and this triumph
              We were never meant to survive.

         ...

         So it is better to speak
          remembering
           we were never meant to survive.

       AUDRE LORDE, A Litany for Survival (1978)

11.7 Snapshot

Combining alliteration, onomatopoeia, and anaphora may produce interesting effects in a poem, especially if it does not have a fixed rhyme scheme, as in Emily Dickinson's poems. Dickinson always combines perfect and slant rhymes with sound effects, presenting various forms of giving unity and balance to the poems. In the poem "I heard a Fly buzz when I died" the poet blends onomatopoeic sounds with alliteration, causing expectation. By bringing together the onomatopoeic sound 'buzz,' and the repetition 'see to see,' the poet produces a certain suspension in the last line of the poem. The buzzing of the fly interrupts the stillness of the moment, creating movement and questioning death.

In the poem, 'Winter in my room,' the repetition of the words "warm" "worm" and "worm" in the first lines sounds uncanny, giving the idea of sameness and uniformity, causing disturbance and disgust. As the poem unveils that the worm is a snake, the onomatopoeic sound hisses confirms that the worm is now dangerous and causes fear. However, in revealing that the snake has speckles, the repetition of the /s/ sound with the image of speckles breaks the idea of danger and the seriousness of the enemy, creating a satiric tone. The poem ends with repetitions of /d/ sounds in the words 'distant' 'down' and 'dream,' slowing down the rhythm, ending the narrative with the pace of children's story where we use to hear sentences like '*in a distant land lived a . . .*'

Dickinson's poem mixes satiric images of snake speckles and the irony of a worm's transformation into a snake to emphasize that the idea of a monstrous worm-snake running after someone from town to town only makes sense in children's stories and bad dreams.

11.8 Practice

> **It's your turn**
>
> Read the poems in this section and find examples of
> alliteration and anaphora. Rewrite your poems and in-
> corporate sound effects.

11.9 Poets

T. S. Eliot (1888 -1965)

was one of the representatives of the modernist move-
ment. Born in Missouri, he moved to England in 1914
at the age of 25.Eliot first attracted widespread attention
for his poem "The Love Song of J. Alfred Prufrock" in
1915, which was received as a modernist masterpiece. It
was followed by some of the best-known poems in the En-
glish language, including "The Waste Land" (1922), "The
Hollow Men" (1925), "Ash Wednesday" (1930), and Four
Quartets (1943).

Audre Lorde (1934 – 1992)

was an American writer, feminist, womanist, librarian,
and civil rights activist. She was a self-described "black,
lesbian, mother, warrior, poet," who "dedicated both her
life and her creative talent to confronting and addressing
injustices of racism, sexism, classism, and homophobia.
As a poet, she is best known for technical mastery and
emotional expression, as well as her poems that express
anger and outrage at civil and social injustices she ob-
served throughout her life.

Reference

Sontag, S. *On Photography*. Picador: New York, 1973.

CUT-UP TECHNIQUE

Our poems formulate the implications of ourselves,
what we feel within and dare make real

Audre Lorde, Poetry is not a luxury

To conclude this journey, I propose an exercise that has helped many poets to reshape and recreate their poems. William Burroughs helped popularize this technique by telling the world he used the cut-up method to shape his poems. Since then, poets, creative writing students and those who love poetry have tried it. What is the cut-up technique?

First, you will select one of your poems, print it, and prepare some scissors, paper and glue. Then, cut it up and rearrange words and verses randomly, looking for new forms to put it together. You can experiment a number of ways of mixing ideas, images, and sounds. As you decide how you want to reorganize your work, glue the new verses on the paper.

Finally, pick some pens, read your work, crossing out every unnecessary word. Linguistic economy is crucial here. Read the poem again, reshape, edit, clean, and polish it. Type the poem again, print it, and compare it with the first version.

INDEX

Made in United States
Orlando, FL
27 April 2025

60810608R00109